How to Choose and Use
Bench Planes and Scrapers

How to Choose and Use

Bench Planes and Scrapers

John English

Linden Publishing

Fresno

To Meg

Published by Linden Publishing
2006 South Mary
Fresno, California 93721
559-233-6633 / 800-345-4447

To order another copy of this book, please call
1-800-345-4447.

Editor: Kent Sorsky
Cover design: James Goold
Photography: John English, except where noted.
Design and layout: Maura J. Zimmer

ISBN 978-1-933502-29-8

Printed in China on acid-free paper.
135798642

Woodworking is inherently dangerous. Your safety is your responsibility.
Neither Linden Publishing nor the author assume
any responsibility for any injuries or accidents.

Library of Congress Cataloging-in-Publication Data

English, John.
  How to choose and use bench planes and scrapers / by John English.
     p. cm.
  Includes bibliographical references and index.
  ISBN 978-1-933502-29-8 (pbk. : alk. paper)
  1. Planes (Hand tools) 2. Woodwork. I. Title.
  TT186.E57 2010
  684'.082--dc22
                  2009040986

Table of Contents

Foreword

I was honored when John asked me to preface this book and surprised that his request sent my thoughts back to the '60s, when I first gave myself over to our craft. Although my ambition was to make beautiful, long-lived things as expeditiously as possible, I was dismissively ignorant about hand planes. The idea of them just held no appeal. They seemed imprecise, labor intensive and expensive. Romantic, I guess, but impractical. Worthwhile, maybe, for their faintly musty cachet, and only then with an oohing and aahing audience. They were antithetical to the speed and uniformity I sought from the machinery I possessed or coveted. As my knowledge grew, those objections faded and now when a novice asks where to begin, I usually suggest that they learn to sharpen, adjust, and control a low-angle block plane and a spare blade shaped by an alternative grind.

When he invited this introduction, John offered that I might cite Sam Maloof and James Krenov, both of whom we each knew from their writings, teaching workshops, and our visits to their studios. Each passed away in 2009, so it seems fitting. We loved Sam's generosity and "Git'er done" mentality, but the only plane I ever saw in his work

area was a neglected side-handled scraper. I once overheard him deflect a question about hand planes, saying a well-sanded surface is at least as smooth as one that is planed. I've thought many times about that remark. Each method of smoothing reveals completely different truths about wood, warm and soft or thrillingly clear, and even the blind can tell them apart.

Krenov, though, trained hand plane Jedis. Behind his back we students knew him as Obi-Wan and joked that in his kit he hoarded

part of a sheet of 600-grit garnet paper that he'd carried out of Malmsten's* in the '50s. Jim's disciples learned what sharp is, how to achieve it, and how to make excellent wooden planes. What I witnessed and experienced, though maybe can't prove, only demonstrate, is that such planes can be torqued and sprung in the course of a pass to produce astonishing subtlety and precision.

Enough, though, of lives and times gone by. Your day approaches and before I yield the floor, here are three things you should hear. First, ownership of a tool is about your relationship with it, and how you've shaped it and yourself through your understanding. You can't buy what you want to be. Secondly, antique tool collectors' clubs are full of generous, kind, knowledgeable people who are eager to share what you want to learn. Their meetings are also the best source for the useable, not-so-collectible pieces I think you ought to be interested in. Lightly battered and worn tools are usually cheaper, feel better and,

to my eye, are more beautiful than sparkling crisp new ones. Finally, a strong magnifying lens is wonderfully useful. Mine came from a $2 garage sale home movie projector. I keep it in a little jar and am still amazed by what it reveals about tools and the work, too. Your perceptions rather than your work or possessions are where you really live, so focus is important.

Mark Koons
Wheatland, Wyoming
October 2009

Mark Koons is an accomplished studio artist and a member of The Furniture Society whose work is represented in museum collections and fine art galleries.

* Ed. Note: A design school run by Carl Malmsten in Stockholm, Sweden, where Scandinavian design was born and where Krenov studied for two years.

Introduction

The word "plane" has a lot of meanings. The first one in Webster has nothing to do with hand tools. It describes a plane as "a flat surface on which a straight line joining any two points on it would wholly lie." The second definition in the dictionary concerns an abbreviation of airplane, and the third is "a tool consisting of a block with a projecting steel blade, used to smooth a wooden or other surface by paring shavings from it." The editors made no mention of the fact that woodworkers often sweat blood trying to make that third plane create the first one.

Hand planes can be intimidating, but as soon as somebody makes the effort to learn even a little about them, they become an addiction. One of my students is a former mathematics professor who took up woodworking well into his retirement years. Our most recent project together was a cherry blanket chest for his grandchild. When the lid didn't close perfectly, I silently handed Max a small block plane to trim the edge above the hinge mortises. For a fleeting moment his eyes wandered to a shelf full of power sanders, and in the split second it took him to decide on the hand plane, I believe he became a woodworker.

Many of us are initially overwhelmed by the mystical, romantic nature of hand planes.

What Max discovered is that, with a little instruction, we can banish the mystery and still keep the romance. The instructions in this book will take you through tuning up a hand plane, sharpening the iron (blade) and then using the tool. While the instructions are functional, the experience that they eventually deliver is unequivocally poetic.

There is a widespread belief among woodworkers that they should be using hand planes, and that there is something special about their use, and consequently a vague sense of loss when planes are not part of the experience. But the advent of belt sanders, jointers and thickness planers has coincided with a generational metamorphosis in occupations. Our fathers and grandfathers knew how to use hand tools because they had no option, and because their jobs often required such skills. Today's woodworkers are overwhelmingly hobbyists with both the income and the opportunity to buy "appliances" that take the work out of woodworking.

Unfortunately, those same machines also take much of the joy.

Many woodworkers believe that learning how to sharpen an iron is all that stands between them and the use of inherited, bought or found planes. This abbreviated path can lead to troubling results such as chipping, stuttering and gouging that can ruin a piece of work (and a woodworker's enthusiasm) in seconds. When one understands how to set the iron and tune the tool, the use of a well-adjusted bench plane can be mesmerizing.

Carpenters and case builders have been using hand planes to work wood since the beginning of the Iron Age, some three thousand years ago. The tools have hardly changed since Roman times, and yet we still imbue them with mystique. In truth, they are nothing more than simple devices that hold a blade at a certain angle, yet gifted people who program computers, perform surgery or fly

airplanes are all equally intimidated by them. After an instructor at the Black Hills School of Woodworking, where I teach, explains bevels and depth settings, any one of our students can handle a plane within minutes. And once they peel a single thin shaving, they are hooked for life.

There's a widespread feeling that the proper use of hand tools is a sound measure of skill. It would probably be more accurate to say that the use of hand tools contributes to, rather than merely quantifies, one's ability. There are some highly skilled woodworkers who never reach for a plane, but they are usually specialists who are involved in production work. For those of us to whom each project is unique, planes are a gift from the gods. They are personal, encouraging the builder to regard wood as more than a mere commodity. No two boards in nature are identical, and planes allow us to deal with their unique vagaries.

This is a book for the average woodworker. It's a simple, straightforward shop manual for people who own a few bench planes and would like to know how to use them. Working wood with hand tools is one of the most satisfying, relaxing and rewarding activities available, and adding planes to a woodworking

regimen will augment it in several ways. Power tools are noisy, dusty and aggressive, all of which get in the way of a quiet, productive day in the shop. Planes are peaceful.

When we plane the face or edge of a board, we slice across cells, exposing a multitude of voids. When we sand, we fill up those voids with dust, the residue of crushed and abraded cell walls. As a finish is applied, the difference is immediately obvious. A planed surface has a deep, rich, translucent quality that is missing in a sanded piece.

Planes also bring art to the craft. We scarcely look at the surface of a board that has passed through a thickness planer, but we are intimately aware of every bump, knot, grain and oddity in a board that has been hand planed. This makes for better material choices, because a heightened awareness of color and grain translates into parts that are better matched visually.

And planes offer superior control. They remove as little as we like, letting us adjust a part for a perfect fit. Sanders bring aggression where planes deliver finesse. If we follow Max's lead and allow a little knowledge to banish the mystery, the rewards of using hand planes are both immediate and lasting.

Let the romance begin.

Chapter 1

Bench Planes: Block, Smoothing, Jack and Jointer

The most common and recognizable hand planes are called bench planes. They are a great addition to the workshop because they are cordless, they create shavings instead of fine dust, and they're quiet. Best of all, used bench planes are widely available and very inexpensive. Most can be tuned for free, and upgraded for the cost of a decent iron (blade).

A bench plane's length is its most important feature, as it determines both how the tool is used and what task it is most suited to perform. There is a distinct relationship between the length of a plane body and its width, so standard sizes have been developed over the past few centuries. There is another relationship at work with planes, too: The largest plane, the jointer, is usually used on the thin edges of boards, while the smallest smoothing plane is used on the wide faces of boards.

Bench planes make boards flat, square and straight. Their primary function is to make stock ready for joinery. Bench planes, especially the smaller ones, can also be used to finesse a joint, chamfer or round over an edge and help in many other ways, but their primary function is simply to ready stock. Boards that come directly from a sawmill have rough surfaces, meandering edges, maybe a twist or a bow, and bench planes traditionally have reduced these characteristics to deliver straight, flat boards with parallel surfaces and edges.

Today, a jointer and a thickness planer handle much of this process. Boards come to the workshop already planed and straight-lined (where at least one edge has been ripped straight), or the woodworker owns the machines and he or she can joint and plane stock as needed.

Bench planes range in size from short block planes (lower left) *used to trim end grain and chamfer edges, to long jointer planes* (2nd from right) *that can be more than two feet long.*

Affordable machinery has most certainly lightened the workload for hand planes, but it will never eliminate them. For example, boards with figured grain tend to tear out when planed by a machine, especially if there's any exposed end grain. A hand plane can follow the grain.

Hand planes are safer and more convenient than machines for tasks such as trimming an edge for a perfect fit or working parts that are too short to run safely through a planer or a jointer.

More often than we care to admit, a board needs to be shaved, coped or scribed for a perfect fit. It's difficult to rig a machine to make such a cut, but a hand plane can fix the problem in a few seconds. When a single part needs to be worked, it's quicker to reach for a plane than to set up a machine. And at other times, a part is too short to be run across a jointer or planer safely, and a hand plane is the perfect answer. One can even lock a hand plane upside-down in a bench vise and work very small parts.

When a woodworker has sharp, well-tuned planes available, the planes will present themselves as the solution to a thousand small challenges. Without them, we tend to fluff a little, or reach for a sander. With hand planes, our work becomes precise, crisp and professional.

Size Matters

In the first half of the twentieth century, bench planes were widely available in a full range of sizes: block, smoothing (No. 1, No. 2, No. 3 and No. 4), jack (No. 5), fore or try (No. 6, halfway between a jack and a jointer), and jointer planes (No. 7 and No. 8). They range in length from about 4" to 24", depending on the manufacturer. One other plane should probably be included here. The scrub plane removes a lot of material quickly because it has a narrow, curved blade. It is usually used before the smoothing planes.

Some of the bench planes are available in ¼ or ½ sizes, too. These generally are the same length as their whole number peer, but the iron is a different width. For example, the cut made by a No. 5 is 2" wide, but a No. 5½ leaves a 2⅜" wide track, while the iron on a No. 5¼ is only 1¾" wide.

Today, the more affordably priced lines are restricted to just block planes, No. 4, No. 5 and No. 7, with some manufacturers adding a No. 3. The numbers are from an old Stanley system that has been adopted by most of the industry, and the smaller array of choices reflects the way in which woodworking has become more mechanized. A good starter set for the modern woodworker would be a couple of block planes (one standard and one low angle), a No. 4 smoother, a jackplane and a decent scraper, such as Stanley's No. 80.

Stanley Bench Plane Dimensions

	Length	Width	Notes	Bevel
Bench Planes				
No. 1	5½"	1¼"	Smoothing	Down
No. 2	7"	1⅝"	Smoothing	Down
No. 3	8"	1¾"	Smoothing	Down
No. 4	9"	2"	Smoothing	Down
No. 4½	10"	2⅜"	Smoothing	Down
No. 5	14"	2"	Jack	Down
No. 5¼	11½"	1¾"	Jack	Down
No. 5½	15"	2¼" to 2⅜"	Jack	Down
No. 6	18"	2⅜"	Fore/Try	Down
No. 7	22"	2⅜"	Jointer	Down
No. 8	24"	2⅝"	Jointer	Down
Block Planes				
No. 9	8¼" to 10"	2"		Up
No. 9¼	6"	1⅝"		Up
No. 9½	6"	1¾"		Up
No. 9¾	6"	1¾"	Rear handle	Up

As skills improve and experience accumulates, craftsmen often begin to collect old planes, or invest in top quality new ones. One of the first new acquisitions is usually a jointer or fore plane. These large tools can be tricky to handle, especially for smaller people, but they do a lot of work quickly.

From block to jointer, the length of a plane is all-important. A long plane rides on the high spots and doesn't dip into the valleys, so it does a much better job of truing a board than a short plane. A short plane will follow contours, while a long body tends to level out the highs and lows. Each has specific applications, as we shall see.

The most useful set of basic planes includes a standard and a low-angle block plane, a No. 4 smoother and perhaps a No. 5 or even a fore plane for dressing edges and flattening wider boards.

Block Planes

The smallest of the bench planes, these are used to chamfer and round over the edges of boards, to trim end grain, and to do small jobs where other tools simply can't fit. Good carpenters carry a block plane in a tool belt or pocket, and use them for everything from paring shims to sharpening pencils. Some furniture builders have even been known to take block planes to the lumberyard, to see what's under the rough surface of high-priced, un-planed boards. (Ask for permission!)

Block planes are distinct in that they are the only bench planes with the bevel of the iron (blade) facing up.

Block planes come in two varieties, a low angle version (usually 12°) and a standard one (20°). This measurement refers to the angle at which the iron rests: When the leading edge touches the wood, the angle between the iron and the wood is either 12° or 20°. This angle is often referred to as bedding. The lower the angle, the more comfortable the plane is to hold and use. A 12° bed on an iron that has been ground and honed to a standard 25° bevel means that the metal meets the wood at 37° (12 plus 25). Most of the other bench planes (with their bevel facing down) have an iron set at 45°, so a low-angle plane slices into the wood at a 8° smaller angle.

The small size of a block plane combines with its low-angle iron to deliver cuts that are generally smooth and free of tear-out. A block plane is less likely than a larger plane to chatter, because the flat back of its iron rests directly against the body of the plane (actually, against the back of the throat). While they are usually pushed, block planes are small enough to pull in the manner of Japanese planes, without giving up too much control. The standard (20°) block plane is more suited to long grain, like that found on the edge of a board, while a low angle

Because of the low angle (12° or 20°) that the iron assumes in a block plane, the cutting edge is inserted with the bevel up. When the bevel is 25°, the cutting edge meets the wood at 37° or 45°.

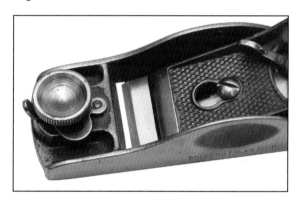

The iron in a bench plane is normally bedded at 45°, and sometimes more (up to 60°). Because of this, the bevel faces down—otherwise the combined angle would be too steep.

A low-angle block plane with a 12° bedding and a 25° bevel meets end grain at 37°. A standard block plane, however, usually beds the iron at 20° and meets end, side or face grain at 45°.

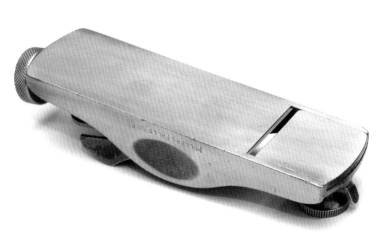

An adjustable throat means that the opening through which the shavings travel can be closed to create a minimal opening. A small opening helps break and curl the wood before it can start a split that travels into your workpiece.

block plane works better on end grain cuts. A standard bed also handles busy, figured grain better. When it comes to figure, the higher the angle the better. Later on, we'll look at specialty planes with almost vertical scraping blades that work remarkably well on figured grain.

Low-angle block planes (where the iron lies at about 12°) usually have adjustable throats. On such a plane, the section of the sole (bottom of the plane) that lies in front of the iron can be moved back and forth, to create a larger or smaller opening. A large opening and a deeper cut combine to deliver better coarse cuts, while a small opening and a shallow cut (that is, a very thin shaving) are used to take fine cuts. This ability to switch between fine and coarse work adds a great deal of versatility to the simple block plane.

When to Use a Block Plane

1. Trimming End Grain

It's counterintuitive to think that a blade can cut across exposed end grain without tearing the wood to shreds. However, a well-tuned block plane can do the job with ease. There are a few elements to the technique that, if followed religiously, can dramatically improve performance. The first of these is to be sure

End grain sticks straight up, so the fibers along the back edge of the board will tear away unless they are slightly chamfered before the cross-grain cut is made. This chamfer needs to be renewed periodically.

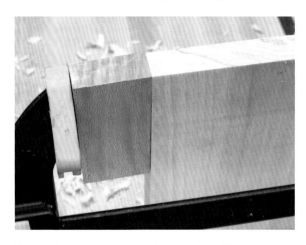

End grain tear-out also can be moderated by dampening the wood with a cloth soaked in water or mineral spirits. Then clamp a sacrificial board to the outfeed side of the cut.

When a plane is held at a slight skew (about 15°), the width of the cut is a little smaller but the slicing action increases, delivering a cleaner cut.

that the iron is razor sharp. Refer to "How to Sharpen a Bench Plane Iron" in Section II for detailed instructions on grinding and honing.

Next, the plane should be well tuned. Again, there are complete instructions in Section II that explains how to flatten the sole and tune the plane.

Once the tool is ready, use it to slightly chamfer the end of the cut. This helps prevent tear-out at the end of each pass. The chamfer will need to be renewed periodically as material is removed. An alternative is to clamp a piece of scrap wood to the end of the cut. Another option is to dampen the end grain with water (some serious woodworkers prefer using mineral spirits, but water works fine). To do this, soak a cloth and dab it onto the end grain, rather than immersing the wood in water. The work is now ready for a first pass, and this is done holding the plane at a slight skew (about 15°), so that it slices rather than tears the grain. If there's any chatter or too much resistance, retract the iron for a lighter cut.

2. Removing Jointer or Planer Marks

Depending on the speed at which a board was fed to the planer or jointer, and the number of knives on the machine's cutter-head, there will be a series of minute, parallel ridges running across the wide face of a board. They usually show up really well when the first coat of stain or finish is being applied. A more serious visible defect is a deeper and less regular pattern of marks known as chatter, and this is the result of poor maintenance or lack of control during the cut. To see these "mill marks," expose the board to a raking light and sight across it. By

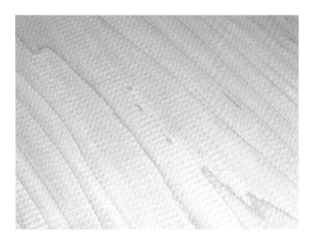

It's disappointing to apply a finish and discover mill marks (parallel lines left by the jointer or planer). Use a raked light to reveal them, a pencil to highlight them, and a sharp card scraper to eliminate them.

Nothing works as well as a sharp, well-tuned block plane to remove chatter along the edge of a board. By taking very thin shavings, the plane removes high spots in the ridges without reshaping the workpiece.

A sharp, low-angle block plane set for a thin cut creates a crisp, clean chamfer (45° angle) along the edge of a shelf, stile or rail in less time than it takes to set up a router with a bearing-guided bit.

A block plane can create an almost perfectly rounded edge in just a few seconds. Take several successive passes, angling the blade a few degrees left or right with each pass.

using the edge of a pencil lead (rather than the point), the ridges can be "painted," so they are more visible.

While a scraper plane works best to remove mill marks on the wide faces of a board, a well-tuned block plane (with a standard angle) is the ideal tool for cleaning chatter from the edges of boards. Set the iron to take a very thin shaving. The first couple of passes may look like they're not removing any stock, but in fact they are shaving the tops of the ridges. Be patient. If the iron is set too aggressively, even one pass along the edge could throw it off square (change it from 90°).

3. Dressing Edges

While bearing-guided chamfering and round-over bits chucked in a router do a great job of breaking edges, they take time to set up, make lots of noise, create fine dust and usually remove too much material. They're also unable to reach into corners. A block plane can deliver a delicate chamfer on the edge of a shelf, stile or rail in a few seconds, with absolute control and a sharp, handsome aspect. Set the plane for a very small cut, check for errant grain that may tear out, and make a practice pass on scrap wood to judge the effect of the cut.

Rounding over an edge is almost as easy. Begin with a pass at 45° (that is, a chamfer cut), and follow up with several passes to the right

The end grain on less-than-perfect miters can be dressed with a sharp block plane. The trick is to begin at the closed end of the joint and take very small cuts until the open end closes tight.

After hanging flush (inset) cabinet doors, the gaps can be evened with a sharp block plane. To help a door close properly, you may need to pare a little bit more from the back of the edge than the front.

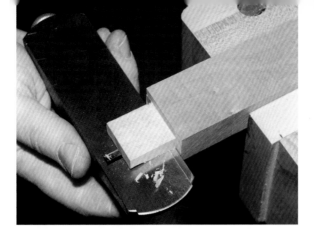

A block plane set for a thin cut can work across the grain on tenon cheeks to create a perfect fit in the mortise. The trick is to maintain uniform thickness so that you don't create a wedge-shaped tenon.

When using a block plane to pare the end grain on exposed dovetails, work from the edge of the board toward the middle. The plane should travel on a slight diagonal to avoid tear-out.

and left, angling the plane another 10° or so each time. Practice on scrap to judge the effect. A light sanding with fine (320 grit) sandpaper delivers a smooth, pleasing radius.

4. Tweaking Joinery

After cutting all eight miters on a picture frame, it's disappointing to find that the saw was off half a degree and the accumulated error has left the frame with four very slightly open miters. By using the end grain planing technique described above, the problem is easy to fix. Use a try square to mark pencil lines where the cuts should be, clamp the work to a bench or in a vise, and work from both ends of the miter toward the middle, to avoid tear-out. This is just one example of how a block plane can tweak joinery, and here are a few more. Flush cabinet doors can be trimmed in a few minutes with a block plane, so that they have the same reveal on each of the three unhinged edges. The cheeks of a tenon can be pared with a block plane for a perfect fit in its mortise, without having to re-chop the mortise or set up a tenoning jig on the table saw. The excess material on assembled dovetails can be worked away in seconds with a block plane: just cut in from the corners of each tail at a diagonal to avoid tear-out. And the ends of through tenons can be smoothed to a clean, pleasing surface after they are assembled to their mortises, simply by cutting across the grain.

Clean up through tenons by working your way around the protrusion using a plane with a tight mouth and a thin cut. Shave the endgrain in several directions, to avoid tear-out.

Smoothing Planes

Designed as the last tools used when flattening the wide faces of boards, smoothing planes include No. 1, No. 2, No. 3 and No. 4. The first couple of these are very small planes that are rarely used anymore and indeed are somewhat difficult to find. Of the others, the No. 4 is the most common, but Lie-Nielsen makes a beautiful bronze bodied No. 3 for smoothing smaller stock. The company describes it as "a perfect tool for when you have a lot of smoothing to do but the pieces are not large. Made just a bit smaller than a No. 4, the No. 3 is designed to be less tiring and easier to use for longer stretches. Construction and design are the same as all the other Bedrock-pattern Lie-Nielsen planes, although here you have a choice of a ductile iron body or a heavier one of solid bronze."

That description says a great deal about smoothing planes in general. Smoothing panels with a hand plane can most definitely be tiring, especially if one is working on a whole kitchen or a similar project with lots of doors. Sometimes it's best to use machines to get most of the way there, and then switch to a smoothing plane to complete the job. The second salient point was the choice between an iron and a bronze body. In planes, stability is key. The weight/mass/density of the tool really makes a difference in eliminating chatter.

The Bedrock pattern referred to above was introduced by Stanley in 1900, and was a marketing concept built on the idea of bedrock being a completely stable foundation upon which to build. The idea, of course, was that the company's planes were also unquestionably stable. The concept came from an improvement patented a few years earlier by Justus Traut, the company's chief engineer, who registered almost 100 patents between 1865 and 1908. In this case his innovation was a radical improvement on the traditional frog, which is the metal bed upon which the iron rests. For the previous four decades, Stanley's line of Bailey bench planes had been the state of the art. For more on the

Lie-Nielsen Toolworks

By far the most common of the smoothing planes is the No. 4. This is the ideal tool for cleaning up after a jack or jointer when flattening wide boards. The No. 1, 2, and 3 planes work well on smaller workpieces.

Stanley-Bailey line of hand planes, see the box at right.

The workhorse of smoothing planes, the metal No. 4 is very easy to find both new and used. There are also smoothing planes with wooden bodies, and some transitional planes (with metal upper bodies attached to wooden soles), but the iron plane is by far the most popular.

When to Use a Smoothing Plane

Woodworkers reach for a No. 4 when the wide face of a board needs to be worked just a little. If the board needs a lot of work, a longer plane is used first to reduce the number and severity of the ridges and valleys. (A jack or fore plane can precede the smoothing plane, and many artisans will employ a scrub plane before those. We'll talk more about all of these options later in Chapter 8.) The smoothing plane is especially useful when a jointer or thickness planer has left mill marks on the face of a board. However, it also serves

History of Hand Planes
Bailey, Leonard (1825-1905)

Responsible for Bailey, Defiant, Victor and Stanley planes, engineer Leonard Bailey was a giant in the plane making industry. Many of his innovations are still incorporated into modern bench planes. He began life as a woodworker, building cabinets in Boston, but soon opened his own toolworks, Bailey, Chaney & Co. His first tool patent was issued in 1855, and twelve years later he patented the familiar design still used today with its cast body, large tote, forward knob, iron set at 45° on an adjustable frog, and the blade held in place by a cap iron, which he also invented. Four years after the war, in 1869, Bailey went to work for Stanley Rule and Level Company, which was the beginning of a turbulent but very creative relationship. Six years later, over a dispute about a new plane created by Stanley's in-house engineer Justus Traut, Bailey quit the company and opened the Victor factory. He spent most of the next few years in court battles with Stanley over copyrights and patents. In the late 1870s he moved the Victor process to Rhode Island and added the Defiance line, but his defiance of court orders never left him a victor in the ongoing battle with Stanley. In 1880, the company became the sole distributors for Victor, and four years later they shut it down.

Beth Sundberg / davistownmuseum.org

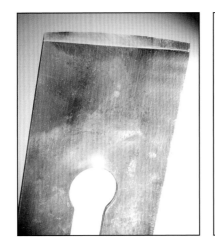

(left) *A very slight bow in the leading edge of a plane iron (called a crown or sometimes a crest) prevents the sharp corners from digging into the board and leaving scratches.*

(right) *For woodworkers who are seeking a flatter, more even cut, the crown can be replaced by a very slight rounding of the corners, known as a radius. A chamfer (shown) is even quicker to apply than a circular radius.*

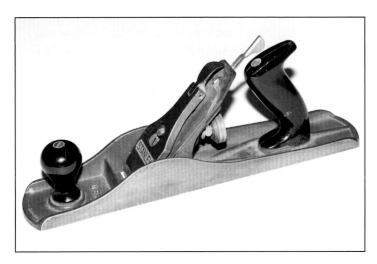

The most useful plane in the workshop is the jack, which received its name from the phrase "Jack of all trades." It is used in carpentry, joinery, casework, and furniture building.

well to dress a surface where the builder wants to leave the subtle and almost invisible texture of hand planing on a board.

Experienced woodworkers sharpen the iron of a smoothing plane with just the hint of a bow to the leading edge. This is called a crown or a crest, and it prevents the square edges of the cutter from leaving two parallel scratches, or tracks. Essentially, the corners of the iron are rounded slightly. There are two opinions on this. The more traditional view is that the entire edge is worked to create a long, very gentle arc (like an understated scrub iron). The other way to work the iron is to just radius the corners. This requires a more exacting bedding of the iron, so that the flat part of the leading edge is absolutely parallel to the work. The long, gentle arc is more forgiving.

Jackplanes

In Shakespeare's England, a "jack of all trades" was a man who could show competency in several of the construction arts. Sometime during the eighteenth century, a cynical wag added the qualifier, "and master of none", turning a positive description into a negative one. However, the original phrase was most definitely a form of praise that was used to describe a skilled artisan. In terms of hand planes, the "jack of all trades" is about 15" long and it, too, performs well in several situations. It acts as a jointer or even a smoother in a pinch, and it is light enough to tote to a jobsite and even carry up a ladder. Since the end of the nineteenth century, countless jackplanes have been used every day in America to fit entry or passage doors, tweak post and beam joinery and perform a myriad tasks that larger or smaller planes were designed to complete. Light and short enough to find its way onto a scaffold or a roof truss, the jackplane also is long and heavy enough to make short work of straightening a board. These versatile tools are the choice of framing and finishing carpenters for any work too large for a block plane to handle.

Furniture builders and cabinetmakers, however, are a little more particular.

When to Use a Jackplane

In the woodshop, a jackplane bridges the gap between a scrub plane and a smoothing plane. A scrub has a dramatically rounded iron and is used to remove large amounts of material quickly. It leaves a trail of gouges that can be cleaned up in a two-step process: first with a jack, and then with a smoother.

The jackplane doesn't always have to follow a scrub. Boards that have been planed by a machine often need a very light dressing with a jack, just to remove mill marks. If the iron is gently crested, and the lumber is straight-grained and clear, the use of a smoothing plane can often be avoided. The jackplane takes a 2" wide shaving on every pass, so it is a quick and efficient way to dress the faces of small boards and panels. It also works well to pare the thickness of a panel that won't quite fit into a groove. Removing thin shavings from the back of a raised panel takes only seconds, and it is quieter, cleaner and more satisfying than sanding.

After the rough treatment received by a scrub plane (above), a jackplane can be used on the diagonal to create a flat, smooth surface (below). This surface can then be dressed with a smoother run with the grain.

When a panel won't quite fit into a groove, a sharp jackplane can reduce its thickness along the edges without having to plane the entire panel to a thinner dimension.

Jointer Planes

The No. 7 and No. 8 are the longest, widest and heaviest planes, and machines of the same name (jointers) have essentially replaced them. An electric jointer with a six or eight inch wide cutter and a good fence is a most efficient piece of equipment, and it will edge boards more quickly and reliably than a hand plane. Sacrilege, you say? Actually, it's just realism. Even the most ardent purist will agree that there are times when a machine is a more appropriate choice than a hand tool. Jointer planes are very large and heavy, and as they are usually not equipped with a fence (although one is available), they rely heavily on the artisan's skill and experience. Try holding such a plane at a consistent 90° along the full length of a long board, and it quickly becomes obvious that this hand tool requires practice. A well-tuned electric jointer with parallel beds and a true fence will better serve the needs of a woodworker in most situations. There are, however, some ways in which a jointer can be used to great effect...

When to Use a Jointer Plane

If a project is already assembled and a repair or adjustment must be performed on a long edge, the jointer plane is a natural choice. One example that comes to mind is dressing the damaged edge of a table or desk, as often happens when a piece of furniture is laid on its side. A few passes with a jointer plane delivers a sharp, crisp, straight new edge.

Another great use for the jointer plane is to clamp it upside-down in the jaws of a vise and use it to dress parts that are too short to be passed through a thickness planer or across the table of an electric jointer. Care must be taken in this situation to protect the tips of fingers.

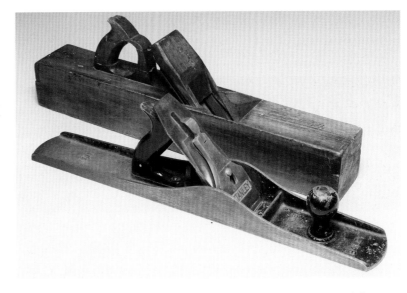

The No. 7 and No. 8 are the longest, widest and heaviest planes. While machines of the same name (that is, jointers) have essentially replaced them in most shops, a well-worn and tuned jointer is still a joy to use.

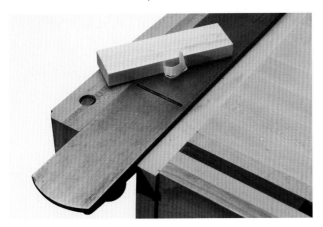

Sometimes a piece of wood is just too short to run across the electric jointer safely. By clamping a jointer plane upside-down in a bench vise, the job can be done safely, quietly, and accurately.

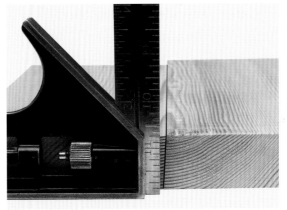

When preparing two boards for edge gluing, they can be clamped together and dressed with a jointer plane. If the cut isn't exactly 90°, open them like a book and the angles will compensate each other.

When preparing two boards for edge gluing, they can be clamped together and dressed with a jointer plane. If the cut isn't exactly 90°, the two boards can be closed up as though connected by a hinge, for a perfect fit.

Of course, there are serious woodworkers who prefer a jointer plane because they don't have the room or the budget for a machine, or they don't have a power outlet on the jobsite, or they simply choose not to live with the noise.

While this book specifically addresses bench planes, it would be impolite to ignore their cousins, the molding planes. These tools are used to cut a decorative or a useful profile on the edge of a board. Sometimes the molded edge was just intended to look nice, while at other times the profile was created to do a job, such as holding glass in a cabinet door. Largely replaced by modern routers, there are still a few manufacturers who dabble in molding planes. The market for these specialized planes is quite small when compared to bench plane sales.

There are two major categories of molding planes. The first is a collection of dedicated planes that hold a single knife that makes only one type of molding. The second category is combination planes, where the cutters can be changed to create different profiles.

Plow planes are often included with molding planes. These are actually a different type of tool, designed to mill grooves and dadoes across boards, rather than shape their edges. Complicated and well-engineered, they are renowned for their beauty. Plow planes were in their glory in the decades after the Civil War, but quickly faded as soon as electric routers arrived on the scene.

Traditionally, finish or trim carpenters (known as joiners) worked primarily with softwoods, while

Simple molding planes from the late 19th century are a great option when starting a hand plane collection for aesthetic reasons, as they can be found in antique store and garage sales at very affordable prices.

furniture builders and cabinetmakers more often used hardwoods. Planes that were intended for use in hardwoods traditionally have a steeper pitch. Bench planes (discussed in Chapter 1) are generally set at 45°, which is known as a standard or "common" pitch. Three other beddings, the York (50°), middle (55°, sometimes called a cabinet pitch) and half (60°), are generally accepted as having been developed in England, although there is some evidence that they were also arrived at independently in Germany. A York pitch is fairly common in molding planes that are intended for softwoods, while the middle and half pitches are used on progressively harder stock.

A steeper pitch reduces tear-out, but it is difficult to use because it generates more resistance, due to its having a scraping rather than a slicing action. This makes it harder to push along the board. This becomes a significant factor when one thinks about the type of work being done. In the 18th and 19th centuries, trim carpenters generally created large, wide profiles on architectural elements such as baseboards and door casings, while furniture builders were more likely to do small molding work on cabinet doors, table edges and so on. As the trim carpenters were often working in softwoods, and on wider boards, and creating longer moldings, it makes sense that they would opt for a lower angle on their molding planes.

Electric routers can cut literally hundreds of profiles, and almost all of those shapes originated as molding plane cutters. Even though the electric spindle router was invented during the 1940s, the vast majority of moldings that predate the Eisenhower administration were hand cut with molding planes. Electric routers replaced these elegant tools in large commercial applications during the 1960s, but hobbyists, collectors and small professional shops have perpetuated a market for molding planes. They are not as common in shops as bench planes, in large part due to

The exquisitely engineered plow plane shown here was made by Hermon Chapin in New Hartford, Connecticut, just before the Civil War, in his Union Factory toolworks.

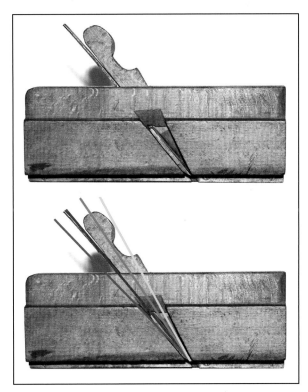

While bench planes are generally set at a common pitch of 45° (red), molding planes like this one are often bedded at York pitch (50°, blue), middle or cabinet pitch (55°, green), or half pitch (60°, yellow), for hardwoods.

History of Hand Planes
Important Figures and Firms in the History of Bench Planes

Modern hand planes are most often made with a cast iron or steel body and a tool steel iron (blade). Cast steel wasn't used widely in Britain until the 18th century, and it took almost another fifty years for it to impact production methods in the United States. The process of making steel in a crucible was discovered and refined by Englishman Benjamin Huntsman in 1742. Although it had been known by other civilizations throughout history, Huntsman's work heralded in the golden age of steelmaking in Sheffield, England.

In the decades leading up to the Civil War, toolmakers and small production shops, primarily in New England and in the Ohio valley, began manufacturing planes that had cast or worked steel and iron bodies, as opposed to traditional wooden ones. These planes, the forerunners of today's bench planes, were immediately popular because their dense bodies provided more heft and impetus (lack of inertia) than the wooden and transitional ones that preceded them. A metal sole also endured less friction, and wear, than wood.

By the end of the war in 1865, Yankee and Ohio mills were turning out cast steel that compared favorably with that of the empire, most notably English steel from Sheffield. Before then, American toolmakers had often resorted to using imported British steel in a domestic forged iron body. With the coming of mass production (including the Bessemer process in 1855 which allowed the mass-production of steel from molten pig iron), planes very quickly began to resemble their current forms. Wooden planemakers, even those in England, either adapted or disappeared, like the notable Cox & Luckman, whose last plane was made in Birmingham in 1876.

Along the way, many ingenious individuals and tool companies contributed key design elements to the new generation of planes. Throughout this book we'll take a look at the makers behind the plane. Just look for the "History of Hand Planes" banner.

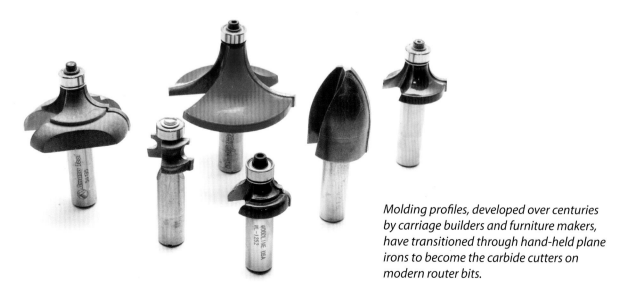

Molding profiles, developed over centuries by carriage builders and furniture makers, have transitioned through hand-held plane irons to become the carbide cutters on modern router bits.

their lack of versatility. Most molding planes cut only a single profile, and they rarely work well on curves (unless made specifically for that purpose). A hand held electric router with a pilot bearing on the bit can follow curves and it will remove material in a fraction of the time taken by a hand plane. It's noisy and dusty and very efficient, but it's not nearly as satisfying. For those woodworkers to whom the journey is as important as the destination, molding planes are a first class ticket.

Combination Planes

Based on a patent issued to senior engineer Justus Traut, Stanley Rule & Level Co. introduced a series of combination planes in 1883 that were still being made as late as the early 1960s. Both the fence and the depth of cut were easily adjustable, and the plane came with as many as twenty-three different profile cutters. It also had spurs, which are small cutters that pre-sliced the grain to help control tear-out.

While molding planes can follow a straight line to create the profile for joints such as a tongue-and-groove, they are rarely capable of working around a curve. Wheelwrights developed compass planes for that task.

At just under a foot long, this versatile tool was small and light enough to fit in a portable toolbox, and it replaced at least a dozen traditional molding planes, making it the cordless tool of choice on building sites across the nation. Copies of it are still being made sporadically, but the originals are widely available (especially on eBay), and they're a better product. Versions dating from after World War I are more useful, because there were several design improvements around that time.

The earlier version of Stanley's combination plane was denoted as No.

Stanley's original combination planes have been copied by many other toolmakers (such as the Montgomery Ward version shown here). These planes came with numerous profile cutters.

45, and a more sophisticated later plane was called the No. 55. Among the cutters available were profiles for nosing, hollowing, beading, fluting, and rounding over. To accommodate them, the plane came with two pairs of steel arms (one long and one short), for working on different widths of wood.

Chapter 3

Joinery Planes: Tongue-and-Groove, Rabbet and Dado

Bench planes are designed to dress the faces, ends and edges of boards. Molding planes mill decorative or useful profiles along the edges of parts, and a third category of planes plows grooves in joinery. These grooves can be across the grain (dadoes), with the grain (grooves), or along the edge of a board (rabbets and tongues). Among the most useful of these joinery planes are the fillister (rabbet), the bull nose (chisel) and the router plane. Once a plane collection has been started, these three usually appear near the top of everyone's wish list. While they're not bench planes, they are extremely common in shops that prefer hand tools, and thereby merit mention.

Rabbet and Fillister Planes

According to Webster's Revised Unabridged Dictionary, a fillister is "the rabbet on the outer edge of a sash bar to hold the glass and the putty." Fillister is also defined by the same source as "a plane for making a rabbet," and the latter (a rabbet) is just a groove that's missing one of its sidewalls. In other words, a rabbet is a ledge that has been cut along the edge of a board, to reduce the board's thickness. Rabbets are used extensively in casework and furniture building, especially where glass is used (windows, mirrors, picture frames), or where frame and panel construction is being employed. A rabbet can reduce the thickness around the edge of a panel so that a thick panel will fit into a narrow groove. In England and in some older American texts, the cut is called a rebate. Rabbets can run with or across the grain.

A fillister plane cuts rabbets along the ends or edges of boards. The depth is controlled by a stop, the width by a fence, and a small cutter known as a nicker slices cross-grain to help reduce tear-out.

One of the defining aspects of a rabbet plane is that the iron (blade) can be set flush to one side of the plane body. This allows the cutting edge to create the wall of the rabbet as it pares away the bottom.

The fence on Stanley's No. 78 Fillister (which controls the width of the rabbet), and the stop (which determines the depth of the rabbet), are each locked in position with a thumbscrew.

One of the defining aspects of a rabbeting plane is that the iron (blade) can be made flush to one side of the plane body . This allows the plane to work right up against the wall of the rabbet.

A fillister is a rabbeting plane that comes equipped with an integral fence and a depth stop. This allows the woodworker to set both the width and the depth of the final cut being made by the plane.

Fillisters also have a small cutter called a nicker that slices across grain, reducing tear-out. By far the most common fillister is Stanley's No.78. It has enjoyed a long and venerable history, and the company still offers a British-made version (the factory stock number is 12-078). It is a cast metal plane with a hollow handle and two positions for the iron. The front position allows the tool to be used as a bull-nose plane, where the cutting edge can reach almost all the way into the end of a groove. (The remaining area can be cleaned up quickly with a sharp chisel.) The back position on the No. 78 is the one that allows for depth of cut adjustments. With the fence locked, the depth set and the iron sharpened, this plane can plow a rabbet in less time than it takes to set up an electric router with a bearing-guided rabbeting bit. And, if the cut is taken across the end of a board (that is, across the grain), the built in nicker will slice the wood and virtually eliminate tear-out.

No. 78 fillister planes can be purchased new, but there is a healthy supply of used ones online at sites such as eBay.com, and these generally sell for about the cost of a good bearing-guided, carbide-tipped rabbeting bit for the electric router.

For a more in-depth discussion of this handy plane, see Chapter 11.

Shoulder, Bull-Nose and Chisel Planes

A shoulder plane is an all-metal plane with a cutter that is the same width as its body, or very slightly wider. It is used to trim the shoulders and cheeks of tenons, and also works well to smooth the bottoms of grooves. A shoulder plane will cut across end grain and pare side grain, so it works well for cleaning up rabbets, too. The iron on a shoulder plane is usually bedded low, and it sits about halfway back in the body. It usually has a turn-screw in back that controls the depth of cut. Several manufacturers make shoulder planes with a detachable front end that can be replaced with a shorter version, in effect turning it into a bull-nose plane (where the iron is almost all of the way forward in the body).

According to Lie-Nielsen Toolworks, their No. 73 all-metal shoulder plane is based on the old Record 073, which in turn was based on a Preston model. The tool is 8¼" long, with a 1¼" blade. The body is cast from ductile iron and the lever cap is bronze. The plane weighs a full 4 lbs, and "the body is precisely ground flat and square, an essential feature for a shoulder plane. The blade is .005" wider than the body, bedded at 18° with a 25° bevel. This is a large tool, but the size gives excellent control even on relatively small work."

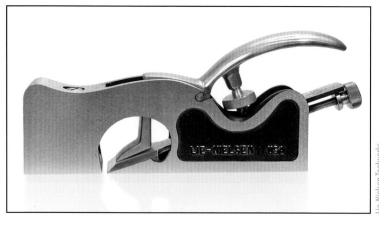

In general, the heavier a shoulder plane's body, the better it cuts across the grain of tenons. Planes such as the large Lie-Nielsen No. 73 shown here can also smooth the bottoms of dadoes.

A version of Stanley's venerable old No. 75 can still be found on the Stanley Tools Web site under the product number 12-075. It's only 4" long and is also widely available as a used item.

A bull-nose is used to work close to the vertical walls of a joint, while still having some support in front of the cutting edge to prevent it from tipping. Stanley's No. 75 bull-nose rabbet plane is just 4" long and was made for almost a century (1879 until 1973). It is widely available online as a used item, and the version shown here once had a Japan coating on the top half of the plane. That top half is secured to the bottom with a single machine screw, and it can be slid back and forth to change the size of the mouth's opening. The chipbreaker is actually the leading edge of the lever cap, which is a cast wedge that is held in place with a tensioned screw. It's not a

History of Hand Planes
Auburn Tool Company

Founded in the last days of the Civil War, the Auburn Tool Company was based in Auburn, New York, between Syracuse and Rochester and about 50 miles from Lake Ontario. Auburn was home to a state prison that was built in 1816, the first in New York and, notoriously, the site of the first electric chair execution, in 1890. The company used prison labor from time to time to manufacture a line of beech molding planes and other woodworking tools. It began as a conglomerate of three other toolmakers (Greenfield, Sandusky and Chapin) who had a goal of controlling prices in the Northeastern U.S. Auburn Tool continued to make planes even after its demise in 1893, when it was incorporated into the Ohio Tool Co. and products were then marketed under that name.

A chisel plane such as this custom model made by Xin Chen of Zen Toolworks, can cut right into a corner. They work well when cleaning up the last bit of waste left by another plane.

very efficient chipbreaker, and the plane clogs often, but as it's only asked to do very light work, this isn't really an issue. Other manufacturer's bull-nose planes are heavier, larger and more suited to paring gross joints than the fine work that the inexpensive yet very useful No. 75 is able to handle.

The essential difference between a bull-nose plane and a chisel plane is that there is support in front of the cutting edge on a bull-nose. When that support is removed, it then becomes a chisel plane, which can work all the way up to the base of a vertical wall. Chisel planes are notoriously difficult to use at first, until one gets used to their action and learns how to set the depth of cut. They are at their best removing the last little bit of material that the bull-nose or shoulder plane missed.

An old-fashioned router plane will clean the bottom of a table sawn groove or a chiseled hinge mortise in only a few seconds, leaving a surface that is perfectly uniform in depth. Shown is a new model from Lie-Nielsen.

Router Planes

A table saw is a handy way to nibble dadoes, grooves or rabbets in plywood or solid stock. But the bottom of a groove made this way is uneven, with long parallel ridges. That's a problem just waiting for an old-fashioned router plane. A router plane can clean the bottom of a groove in seconds, leaving a surface that is of uniform depth throughout its length. It works like a dream when it comes to cleaning up hinge mortises, stopped dadoes and grooves, and jig parts that need a groove milled to a very precise depth.

Most of the modern versions of this old standby are based on the elegantly simple Stanley #71. This plane was made from 1884 until 1973 in the US, until 1993 in Britain, and is now copied (and often improved upon) by several manufacturers. It has a flat base with handles, and the L-shaped cutters come in various widths for different grooves. The depth of cut is controlled with a pair of knurled knobs, and sharpening the cutters is just a matter of dressing the bottom surface. The blade can be turned 180° to protrude beyond the base, and this essentially turns the tool into a bull-nose plane. Generally, three cutters are available: on their much improved and quite beautiful #05P38 version of the original No. 71, Veritas offers ¼" and ½" straight cutters, and a ½" pointed one for general smoothing. They also offer a fence, although making a shop-built one is quite simple.

Many of the Stanley No. 71 router planes available in yard sales and online auctions are missing the band that ties the cutter to the vertical post. I had a local machine shop make a new band for the plane shown here, and it cost about the price of a nice lunch.

There are numerous other joinery planes available, but these three will handle most of the basic jobs that are beyond the scope of bench planes. Together, they make a great start to one's collection of antique planes.

The antique router plane shown here, a Stanley model patented in October 1901, is a good example of how a damaged tool can find new life. The band (oval ring), bolts and knurled knobs have all been replaced.

One of the most gratifying aspects of bench planes is that they reduce the amount of time woodworkers spend sanding. But there's another, quite similar family of tools that can cost as little as two or three sheets of sandpaper, and can almost eliminate sanding altogether. These miracle tools are scrapers.

Indeed, metal and glass scrapers were once the only way to smooth a glue joint or erase a ridge left by a bench plane. Then sandpaper came along, and once somebody figured out how to motorize the task, sanding quickly became a less labor-intensive option than scraping. However, sanding fills the open cells in wood, creates dust, rounds over crisp edges, makes noise and is in general an invasive procedure. Scraping, on the other hand,

slices the face of a board, leaving a surface that will accept a finish beautifully. While shaves (including drawknives and spoke shaves) are extremely useful when shaping a part, scrapers are more adept at preparing a surface for finishing. Two main kinds of scrapers are used in the woodshop: card scrapers and cabinet scrapers.

Card Scrapers

Flat pieces of metal known as card scrapers are used to perform a variety of tasks on hardwoods, such as removing mill marks from a planer, cleaning up excess dried glue along joints, and even trimming dowel pins or glued-on hardwood edging. These tools are often called cabinet scrapers, which is a misnomer. While their faces are flat, card scrapers' edges come in a variety of shapes, so that they can reach around molding and edge profiles as well as working on flat surfaces. The most popular size is a standard rectangle, usually measuring about 3" x 6". Another common shape, the gooseneck or swan, has a gradual French curve that is ideal for cleaning up cabriole legs and other tapered, round or curved surfaces. The third most frequently seen shape is a rectangle with a convex curve on one end and a concave curve on the other. Custom shaped card scrapers can be

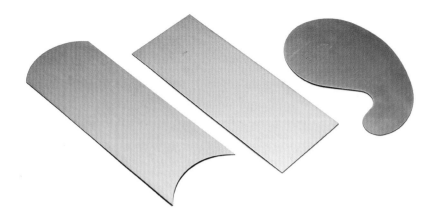

Most manufacturers sell card scrapers as a single item with a rectangular shape, or as a set (usually three) with different shapes that can be used to address moldings and milled profiles.

made from any high carbon steel, such as old band saw or hack saw blades.

Card scrapers are ideal for working on veneer because they are generally less aggressive than a bench or block plane, or a sander, and they also work well to reduce inlays and edge banding. They don't work as well on softwoods as hardwoods, but the results are not bad. In softwoods, they tend to tear out the grain. Card scrapers are made from high quality flexible steel, and the key to success lies in the sharpening process.

Sharpening a Card Scraper

Begin the process by removing any burrs from the wide, flat faces. This is best done on a bench stone (diamonds are the quickest, but oil and water stones also get the job done). Simply lay the scraper on the stone after applying the relevant lubricant (water or oil), and move it in repetitive gentle arcs. You can hear and feel when there is no more resistance and the burr has been removed.

Next, make the edges straight. This is actually referred to as jointing the edge, much as one joints the edge of a board to make it straight. There are numerous options here, the quickest of which is to use a fine belt in a stationary belt sander. This works well if the platen (the steel supporting the belt) is flat, and if the belt travels slowly enough so that it doesn't overheat the metal. An oscillating belt dissipates the heat more effectively, and also

1) The first step in sharpening a card scraper is to use a flat bench stone to remove all vestiges of the old, rolled burrs along its edges. Medium grit diamond, water or oilstones will work.

distributes the wear pattern so the metal edge of the scraper is less likely to work through the abrasive coating, or indeed the fabric backing of the belt. Don't turn on dust collection for the sander, as the hot metal may ignite sawdust in the collector (which usually happens at about

3 AM the following morning!). Wear a dust mask, as fine metal dust can be quite harmful if breathed.

One other method that is actually preferable to sanding is to lock the scraper in the jaws of a vise and use a fine file to dress the edges. Lining the jaws with wood is a good idea, so the vise doesn't damage the scraper. Keep the file level and make several passes along the full length of the scraper. Every now and then, lay a square or other straightedge on the scraper to check for gaps that indicate a low spot along the edge. A strong light behind the scraper will pinpoint problems.

At this stage, artisans who build guitars, violins or work extensively with veneers often grind a bevel on one edge of their card scraper, before burnishing. Cabinetmakers and furniture builders don't go this route, as the beveled scraper will quickly lose its edge.

When the two long edges of a standard rectangular card scraper are straight, it's time to burnish them. (Sometimes the short ends need to be dressed instead, so that the scraper can fit into tight spots.) The idea here is to raise and then turn a burr on each side of each edge, giving you four working edges. This cuts sharpening downtime to a minimum. A burr is the thin edge of steel that actually does the work while scraping. Raising the burr occurs when you rub something harder than the scraper along the edge, rolling a thin fingernail of steel off each edge. Turning the burr means that the fingernail is rolled a little past horizontal to give it a little tooth for scraping.

Burnishing is done with a burnishing tool, a rod of extremely hard steel with a wooden or plastic handle. Burnishers are widely available from hand tool suppliers or they can be ordered

2) If a fine file isn't available, a fine-grit oscillating belt sander can be used to straighten the edges of a rectangular card scraper. The oscillating action helps avoid heat build-up in the metal.

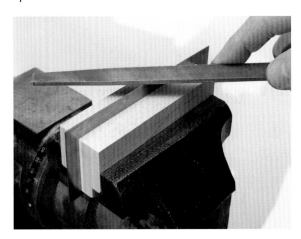

3) The traditional way to straighten a card scraper's edges is to lock the tool in a vise equipped with wooden jaws and use a fine file to dress the edges. If they aren't flat, steel vise jaws can change the shape of a scraper.

4) Low spots along the edge of a scraper will yield high spots on the surface of a board, so it's a good idea to check the edge periodically with a steel square or straightedge.

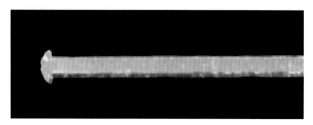

5) With the edges straight, the next step is to roll burrs along them. A burr (shown here in close-up) is a fingernail of steel pushed outwards to create an abrasive hook that does the actual scraping.

6) Apply a thin coat of light oil to the edges of the scraper, hold the burnishing rod in both hands, press down firmly, and then slide it along the full length of the scraper about a dozen times. Be careful with this step: It's easy to slip and cut a finger.

7) After dressing the edges at 90°, tilt the burnishing rod two or three degrees to one side, and take about a dozen strokes. Then, tilt the rod a couple of degrees in the opposite direction and begin to roll the other burr.

online from most woodworking supply sites. After clamping the scraper in a vise, apply a thin coat of machine oil to the edge to be burnished. It works best if you first apply the oil to a rag, and use the rag to spread the fluid along the edge. Fingers used to spread the oil tend to get themselves cut. Grasp the burnishing rod in both hands and slide it along the full length of the scraper's edge, pressing down firmly on the scraper's edge. Keep in mind that the scraper will slice your knuckles if the tool slips, so a solid stance with good balance is essential. Make about a dozen passes while holding the tool horizontal (that is, at 90° to the wide faces of the scraper). Be sure to burnish the full length of the edge: it's tempting to start in the middle and work in both directions, but this delivers a hollow in the middle where the strokes overlap. Personally, I like to remove the scraper halfway through this step and turn it end for end in the vise, to make sure that the strokes are even all the way along the edge of the scraper.

Rolling the burr is next. Tilt the burnishing tool two or three degrees to one side, and take about a dozen strokes. Then tilt the burnisher a couple of degrees in the opposite direction and begin to roll the other burr. Return to the first edge, tilt the burnisher to about five degrees and then repeat the process on each side. At this point you should be able to use your fingers, carefully, to feel a pronounced burr on each side.

Remove the scraper from the vise, rotate it 180° and lock it back in the vise. Now you can burnish both sides of the other long edge, following the process outlined above. When these last burrs feel satisfactory, remove the scraper from the vise and use a dry, clean cloth to wipe off any remaining oil so that it won't contaminate workpieces and spoil a finish.

Woodsmith™ offers a very helpful jig for sharpening and burnishing a card scraper. It can be viewed online at **www.WoodSmithStore.com/cabinetscraper.html**.

Use a Card Scraper

Card scrapers can be tricky at first, and even a little discouraging. However, it only takes a few minutes to master the technique, and once learned it will deliver significant rewards for years to come. Card scrapers perform especially well on tricky, wild grain or high figure, where a bench plane would chip or tear out. They also deliver a cleaner, crisper finished surface than sandpaper can.

The goal here is to produce fine shavings much like the ones made by a well-tuned plane, only they will be much smaller. If the scraper makes only dust, then either it needs to be sharpened or an improper technique is being used. The correct method involves gripping the ends of the scraper firmly with both thumbs on the back and two fingers on the front face of each side. This grip allows the woodworker to flex or bend the metal in a gentle arc. The apex of the arc (the middle of the curve) should be toward the front with the edges of the scraper trailing behind. The arc raises the outside corners and prevents them from digging into the work.

When using a card scraper, grip its ends firmly, place both thumbs on the back and two fingers on each side. Scrape the wood to produce light shavings like those made by a well-tuned plane, only much smaller.

Firmly gripped, the tool is then tilted forward at about a 40° to 45° angle to maximize the cutting effect of the burr. Short strokes work best (the stroke is away from the user), and it's a lot smarter to practice your technique on scrap wood rather than an almost complete project. The stroke should begin lightly, press down somewhat powerfully in the middle, and lighten up again at the end. This has the effect of feathering each cut and blending them together so that no mill marks remain. Pressing down also eliminates chatter. A pull stroke can be used, but it doesn't work nearly as well. And be aware that after a few strokes the scraper will begin to heat up. For this reason, many experienced cabinetmakers like to wrap the scraper in masking tape, leaving about ½" exposed top and bottom. Others keep a tray of cold water handy to dip the steel and cool it. If you opt for cooling the scraper with water, dry the scraper after cooling as neither the steel nor the wood will benefit from residual

It's easy to tell when a card scraper needs sharpening: The worn burr begins to produce fine dust instead of satisfying shavings. Lowering the angle of address often lets the burr catch, allowing you to delay sharpening.

water. One other way to deal with heat buildup is to install the card scraper in a wooden handle, which brings us to cabinet scrapers.

For woodworkers who would like to learn more about card scrapers and see them in action, David Marks of the DIY Channel has produced a DVD on the subject. David maintains that "the scraper is one of the most important hand tools a woodworker can have in his shop." In the DVD, David gives detailed step-by-step instructions on how to sharpen the card scraper; an introduction to water stones and their role in sharpening scrapers; explains how to sharpen the gooseneck scraper; and how to sharpen the Stanley No. 80 Cabinet Scraper (see below). After sharpening those tools, he shows how to use them.

Cabinet Scrapers

Members of the second category of scrapers come with handles. Included are cabinet scrapers, scraper planes, wooden handles that are made to hold card scrapers, and even standard old paint scrapers.

Even though there are some similarities, a cabinet scraper is not the same thing as a scraper plane (which is used to tackle lively grain). Cabinet scrapers have a thinner blade, which is most often bowed a little by a thumbscrew behind the blade, and they lean forward a few degrees.

Among the most popular of the cabinet scrapers is Stanley's No. 80. What distinguishes the No. 80 from handheld card scrapers is not so much the handle, but the base. It is relatively deep from front to back, which means that it rides across the low spots. This is a blessing because it helps one avoid digging holes or trenches in a surface.

The No. 80 is used by gripping both handles, placing your thumbs in the corners behind the blade, and pushing forward (away from the user). It works best when held askew to its travel. That is, the scraper usually follows the grain, but its leading edge is held at an angle to the grain (usually between 30° and 45°).

A No. 80 scraping plane holds the blade at a fixed angle, and its relatively large base offers some stability. Nevertheless, it pays to practice on scrap wood before using this tool on an actual project.

The action is short, repetitive motions, rather than long sweeping ones, and two things control the depth of cut: the set (depth) of the blade, and the thumbscrew at the back. But before one can set the blade, it must be sharpened.

The first step here is to flatten both faces of the blade, removing any burrs. The quickest way to do this is on a series of water or diamond or bench stones. Work down through the grits from coarse to fine. It only takes a few seconds on each stone. Following that, only one face of the cabinet scraper blade is beveled, and the edge of that face is ground to a 45° angle. This can be done on a series of diamond stones, or on a friable wheel. Once the bevel is established, future sharpening takes a lot less time, as then the bevel only has to be honed (touched up), and not completely reground. The advantage to using bench stones in honing is that a wide stone delivers a more consistent edge across the scraper's entire width than a ¾" or 1" wide grindstone. Diamond stones cut much more quickly than oilstones or even water stones, and water stones are pretty soft for this kind of work. Another option is to lock the blade in a vise and reveal the bevel using a file, but this takes practice to be consistent. Using a honing guide on stones or tool rest with a motorized wheel will deliver repeatable results.

I strongly advise against sharpening both long edges on a No. 80 blade, as the second edge will extend past the body and the exposed edge will cut into fingers during use.

Once the bevel is ground, it needs to be honed and polished. This is done by dressing it on a medium grit stone, and then finishing up on a fine grit stone (1000 and 4000 water stones work well).

The No. 80 works best with two thumbs behind the blade housing. The angle of address needs to be skewed a little to allow the wood fibers to slide along the blade as they are sliced from the board.

Begin sharpening the blade of a No. 80 by removing the old burrs on a flat bench stone. Diamond stones are ideally suited to this task, as they cut quickly and stay very flat. Water and oilstones need to be flattened first.

Grind one edge of a scraper blade to 45 °, using a slow, fine stone. While it's tempting, don't grind the second (top) edge, as this exposed sharp bevel may cut fingers during use.

The action needed to roll a burr on a 45° scraper plane blade is a lot less aggressive than that used to form burrs on the 90° edges of a card scraper. A couple of quick passes is usually all it takes.

With the edge prepared, the next step is to draw a burr across it using a burnishing rod or the shaft of a large screwdriver or drill bit. After clamping the blade in a vise (hopefully one with wooden jaws), apply a thin line of oil to the edge, and then roll the burr away from the bevel. A dozen or so passes will usually suffice, and there's no need for great force as the beveled edge is quite thin. The burnishing tool should ride the bevel for the first pass, and then drop a degree or so on each succeeding pass until an even burr has been formed across the entire width of the blade. Working from the center toward each end seems like it would be a good way to go, but that works the middle of the blade twice as much as the ends. Just start on one end and work toward the other. During the last stroke, the tool should be at about 20° from horizontal. Going much further than this tends to make the burr too weak. If you haven't gone far enough, you'll know this as soon as you try to use the tool. If it doesn't cut, it only takes a minute to remove the blade, take a few more passes with the burnisher and re-install it. This is just a matter of experience.

Some woodworkers like to burnish in two steps. They first draw out the burr by burnishing toward the bevel, and then on their very last pass they turn the burr so that it rolls away from the bevel. This is a more traditional method, and there are some arguments for doing it, but it has the net effect of bending the thin steel first in one direction and then the other. This inevitably weakens the edge, and the burr doesn't seem to last very long.

There's no need to round the corners, as the thumbscrew behind the blade bows it so that the corners never dig into the workpiece.

To set the blade height (that is, the depth of cut), place a sheet of inkjet paper on a flat surface such as the cast iron top of a table saw, and place the cabinet scraper on the paper so that the mouth (the opening for the blade) is just off the edge. By letting the blade slide down so it touches the table, only the thickness of a single sheet of paper of the cutting edge is revealed. Tighten the two thumbscrews that hold the blade, and then tighten the single thumbscrew behind the blade to bow the front and create an arc along the cutting edge. Try the scraper. If it doesn't produce shavings, try tightening the screw behind the blade a bit more. Keep repeating these steps until shavings appear.

A cabinet scraper works best if it is held at about a 30° angle to the grain, while still traveling with the direction of the grain. This is called

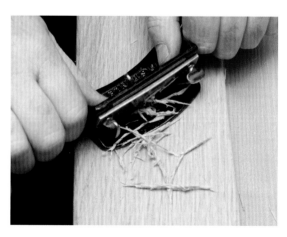

In most species, a scraper plane works best when traveling in the same direction as the grain but with its front edge skewed to maximize the slicing action of the cutter.

skewing. If the skew is to the right and it chatters, then switch the skew to the left and try again. The stroke should begin lightly, pressure should increase in the middle and lighten up again toward the end of the cut. Practice is essential.

The Stanley No. 12

Somewhere between cabinet scrapers and bench planes, Stanley's venerable No. 12 is a cast iron tool with a wooden handle and an inflexible iron, which should categorize it as a plane, except that it does almost exactly the same job as a cabinet scraper. On eBay and in other online marketplaces, this plane is a widely available, heavier and larger version of the No. 80. There is one very big difference between these two tools. The blade on the No. 12 can be tilted back and forth. Instead of resting at a fixed angle, it can be adjusted through a range of angles to suit the job at hand. Originally designed as a veneer scraper, the No. 12 can actually be used for both fine and coarse work, on face and end grain. It does work better on hardwoods than softwoods. It tilts from roughly 15° back (shy of vertical) to 35° forward, a range of some 50°. When the blade has been properly sharpened and is set to lean slightly forward, this plane makes quick work of cleaning up large, wide surfaces on even coarse grained hardwoods. It takes a little experimenting to find exactly the right angle for different grains and wood densities. A good place to start is about 5° forward of vertical. As the burr wears, tilt the cutter forward another few degrees. It's sometimes necessary to lower it a hair, too.

The stroke with a No. 12 is away from the body, with the handle lying closer to the operator than the blade. This tool is so heavy that it hardly needs to be pushed down. This weight, however, works against it at the end of a board where it can tip over the edge. The handle (generally rosewood) is

The blade on a No. 12 can be tilted back and forth from roughly 15° shy of vertical to 35° forward, a range of some 50° that will handle both fine and coarse work in face and end grain.

Work the heavy No. 12 away from the body, skewing the front edge while following the grain. This tool shaves less dense woods such as mahogany and walnut, and has more of a cutting action on coarse grains such as oak.

extremely comfortable, and because it is secured at right angles to the body of the plane, it really helps a woodworker lean into the work. Skewing the plane can help when working certain hardwoods.

Sharpening a No. 12 is very similar to the regimen outlined above for a No. 80 (grind at 45° and turn a burr away from the bevel), except that it really helps to crown the blade. That is, a very slight convex arc on the leading edge prevents the corners from digging into the work, and thus leaving visible trails across a board. On the smaller plane (the No. 80), this is accomplished by tightening a thumbscrew behind the blade to force it into a bow shape. With the No. 12, this isn't an option as there is no thumbscrew. The blade is also much thicker and far more rigid, especially if one heeds the advice of many experienced professionals and chooses to replace the original Stanley blade with one made by Hock (**www.HockTools.com**).

Another family of scraper planes merits special mention. Lie-Nielsen Toolworks offers three planes that are simply exquisite, with the rich feel and exuberant heft of high quality hand tools. Heavy and beautifully made, their small scraping plane, cast in either bronze or iron, is just 5½" long and sports a 1⅜" wide blade. The plane is based on the Stanley 212 (discontinued in 1934), and the blade tilts. Optional toothed blades—for preparing surfaces for veneering and for working exceptionally difficult grains—are available in coarse (18 teeth per inch) and fine (25 teeth per inch). The company offers the following use instructions:

> "The blade angle should be set about 15° forward of vertical. Try adjusting the angle to find optimum performance in various woods. One way to get it close is to take some test passes holding the blade by hand, varying the angle until it cuts best, then hold the blade at that angle against the side of the plane and adjust the frog to match. The beveled faces of the nuts fit into the countersink on the hole in the post to provide a solid lock.
>
> Normally, one pushes the scraping plane from the rear with the knob in the palm. The blade is inserted with a bevel facing the knob. It is best to use a light touch, rather than trying to remove too much material at once, or using too much downward pressure. Too aggressive a cut, including too much downward pressure, will result in chatter. You should be taking light strokes. Often it is helpful to scrape at an angle to the grain, then again from the opposite angle."

History of Hand Planes
Auburn Metallic Plane Company

About the time the wooden planes of the Auburn Tool Company were giving way to new, post-war metal planes, a new company appeared in the city. Nobody made more metal planes in upstate New York during the 1800s than the new Auburn Metallic Plane Company. The company was founded in 1867 by Elliot Storke and it enjoyed immediate success with a line of bench planes based on improvements patented by the Palmer brothers, and sold for less than competing Stanley models. Among the innovations attributed to Auburn Metallic were several improvements in ways to adjust the depth of cut.

This company gave Stanley a run for its money during the early 1870s, but by the end of that decade Stanley's sheer size and overwhelming marketing abilities allowed it to dominate, and the Auburn Metallic Plane Company was dissolved in 1880.

Peter McBride / petermcbride.com

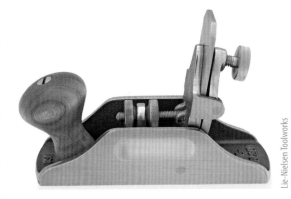

Lie-Nielsen Toolworks

The smallest of three scraper planes from Lie-Nielsen Toolworks, the indisputably elegant 212 features a tilting blade. The inspiration behind its design was Stanley's original No. 212, made during the 1920s.

Lie-Nielsen's middle-sized scraper plane is a fixed-blade version with a full-width 2" blade that allows for work against vertical sidewalls. The stationary blade limits any tendency to chatter, making this the easiest scraping plane for a beginner to use. It has an iron body, a bronze frog, and an overall length of 8⅜".

The largest of the three scraper planes, also based on an old Stanley (the No. 112), has an iron body and measures 9½" long. It weighs in at a considerable 4 lbs. and is great for working large surfaces such as tabletops.

Chapter 5
Plane Construction: Wood, Metal and Hybrids

Plane stocks (bodies) are made with basic materials, wood and iron. Some of the iron has been converted to steel, or had nickel or other metals added. There are a few European planes with plastic body components, but they're not common and, in the opinion of most professional woodworkers, they have yet to prove themselves over time.

For now, the main types of plane body are:

- Cast iron
- Wood
- Infill planes
- Transitional planes

Cast Iron

Cast iron hand planes have been available as mass-produced tools since the late industrial revolution in England, around the middle of the nineteenth century. Before that, and indeed for some time after, individual craftsmen would often fashion their own tools in wood. By the 1860s, Leonard Bailey began to develop a line of cast iron planes that quickly became the industry standard. Affordable, reliable and effective, they revolutionized the jobsite for carpenters and joiners (what we now call trim or finish carpenters). In 1869, the Stanley Rule & Level Co. in New Britain, Connecticut, purchased Bailey's company. Today, the image of a hand plane that jumps to mind is usually a modern Stanley, with its iconic wooden tote (handle) and knob, and a bevel-down iron set at about 45°. This design is almost unchanged from Bailey's original and remarkable concept.

The advantages to cast iron plane bodies are weight, endurance, and accuracy when planing. The heavier a plane is, the more controlled the cut. Metal bodies don't wear over time, so they don't need to be periodically dressed (flattened) in the manner of wooden bodies. They also don't inherit the user's leanings. That is, if a carpenter tends to lean always to the right, a wooden plane will eventually wear down on that side. If a wooden plane hits a particularly hard knot or a piece of embedded lead in a board (a common enough problem when people depended on hunting instead of feedlots), it can become distressed, or chipped. A metal body can withstand far more impact. This durability also comes into play when the sides of the body are asked to run against a fence, as in shooting.

Other than bench planes, certain other plane bodies benefit from being made entirely of metal. These include shoulder planes and rabbet planes such as the Lie-Nielsen No. 10¼, which rely on absolutely square sides to work properly. This 10¼ is the largest rabbet plane made, and it's based on an old Stanley model that was available until the 1940s. Prior to Lie-Nielsen's 212, this model hasn't been made since the Second World War, and never before in the Bedrock format. This wonderful plane has cross-grain nickers to score grain ahead of the iron and reduce tear-out,

(right) *Shoulder planes, which are primarily used for trimming tenons and cleaning out grooves, often have handles that tilt left or right to help them reach into tight spaces.*

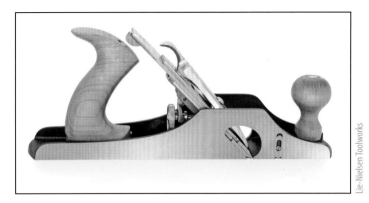

The cross-grain nicker on Lie-Nielsen's No. 10¼ is built into the side of the plane body between the opening and the tote. Its long profile allows for several sharpenings, and the blade is replaceable.

Compass planes like this old Stanley 113 have a flexible sole that can be adjusted to form or pare both inside and outside curves. Before these planes were made, wooden planes of a fixed radius were used.

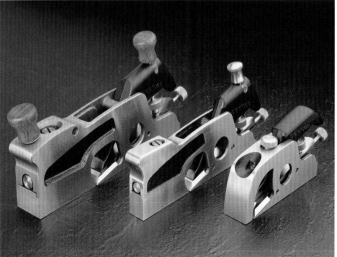

and tilting knobs and handles to allow access in tight spots. It has a ductile iron body, cherry handles and a bronze cap and frog. The cut is 2⅛" wide.

Metal planes also include many specialty tools such as compass planes, including those made by Keen Kutter, Stanley and Union Tool. These are adjustable planes used for forming and cleaning both inside and outside curves. They allowed coopers and carriage builders to work in radii beyond those covered by traditional wooden fixed radius planes.

Shoulder planes are designed to trim the shoulders of tenons so that they fit perfectly into mortises. However, they do a lot more than that. They are ideal for finessing rabbets, the bottoms of grooves and dadoes, the cheeks of lap joints and almost any situation where accuracy in a joint is paramount. A modified version, which is missing the part of the sole in front of the iron, is called a bull-nose plane. This tool is perfect for cleaning out the corners of joinery, but doesn't work too well on wider faces due to the lack of support in the modified sole.

Rabbet planes are usually made of metal nowadays, as traditional wooden bodies tend to wear over time and lose their accuracy. They are not as precise as the lower angled, bevel-up, small-mouthed shoulder planes, and as such are not intended for use within the strictures of a groove.

All Wood Bodies

Beginning with Greek, Egyptian and most notably Roman planes from almost three thousand years ago, joiners and cabinetmakers have always built their own wooden bench planes. The earliest record of mass production was the output of

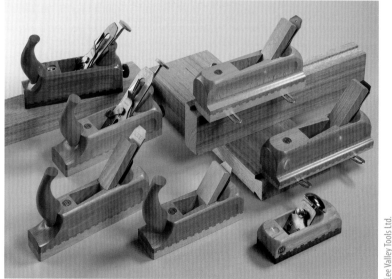

These European style wooden planes, made by the German company E C Emmerich, have beech bodies and use a harder species such as hornbeam or lignum vitae for the sole.

Massachusetts plane maker Francis Nicholson, who operated a factory of sorts from about 1728 until his death in 1753. His workforce consisted of himself and a slave.

Shown here is a selection of E C Emmerich hand planes that are made in Germany. They have a European beech body and hornbeam sole. The iron is held in place with a traditional wooden wedge. The company, based in Remscheid, has been making planes since before the Civil War. The original owner, Friedrich-Wilhelm Emmerich, was a cabinetmaker who made planes for himself. They were so good that the other craftsmen in the shop began to ask him to build planes for them, too. The same family still runs the company today.

The only metal parts in most wooden bodied planes were, and still are, the iron (blade), sometimes a cap iron or chip breaker, and perhaps a few screws to hold a tote (handle) in place. The iron is generally locked in place with a wooden wedge, which is usually but not always in the same species as the stock. A strike, which is a small button or sometimes a knob near the front of the plane, was sometimes made of metal. When struck with a hammer or mallet, the strike is used to adjust the depth of cut, in the manner of Japanese planes. Like Japanese saws, these planes are pulled across the work, delivering great control but requiring a different stance. On the left in the photo is a white oak smoother—unlike original Japanese planes this one has a metal cap iron (chipbreaker).

Shown here are a Japanese smoothing plane with a metal cap iron that replaces the tradition wood wedge, a chamfer plane and a rounding plane (two views) that cuts two radii.

According to Lee Valley, the cut can be increased by simply "tapping the front of the plane with a mallet; to decrease the cut, tap the back of the plane. The high-carbon steel blade will hold a keen edge to achieve tissue-thin shavings, even in difficult woods."

Also shown are a chamfering plane, and two images of a round molding plane that makes two different radius cuts ($3/32$" and $3/16$"). It may require a bit of practice in setting up the blade to achieve the final cut, but once there, it performs remarkably well.

Beech planes often feature a harder species inset into areas of constant wear. On earlier (nineteenth century) planes, this wear-resistant inlay is almost always either apple or boxwood.

Following the European lead, American wooden-bodied planes were and are still most often made from beech (or sometimes maple and, rarely, birch). While lignum vitae or hornbeam soles are not too common in American planes (E C Emmerich makes a beautiful smoother, the Model No. 111-S, that has a lignum vitae sole and a cherry body), many of the later planes do feature a harder species inset into areas of constant wear, such as along the edge of a fence or a detail profile. In earlier planes, this wear-resistant inlay is almost always either apple or boxwood, the latter being cut from a family of durable, hardy shrubs that are widely available in Central America, Europe and Asia.

This same species was often used to make threaded wooden rods on more elaborate molding planes. Sometimes, in later planes, one sees lignum vitae or other extremely hard and stable species used as an inlay in fences or even soles.

Wooden bodies are common to virtually all types of planes, from block and bench to molding and specialty

History of Hand Planes
Chapin

Hermon Chapin's shop made the highest quality rules, gauges, and hand planes in Connecticut from the 1820s until the end of the Civil War. He worked extensively in beech with applewood and boxwood inserts. Known primarily for elaborate wooden plow planes, his Union Factory was still going strong until the Great Depression, albeit in a new incarnation that had worked its way through several generations and partnerships. In 1929, it was known as the Chapin-Stephens Co. Union Factory, and was still located in the vicinity of Hartford, Connecticut. Inevitably, Stanley Rule & Level purchased the company soon after. Chapin never transitioned to metal planes, but he did work in metal. In 1854, his company letterhead noted that he made "Rules, Planes, Castings, Machinery, Bar iron, Axle Drafts, Crow Bars, &c. &c."

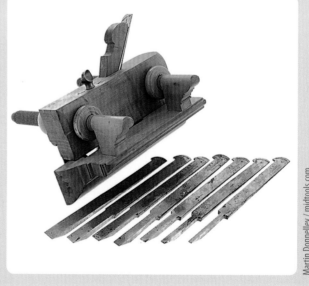

Martin Donnelley / mjdtools.com

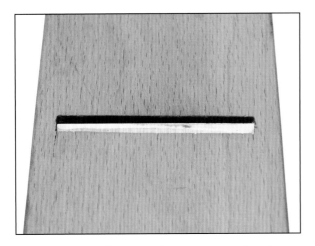

When using a wedge to set the iron in a wooden plane, turn the plane over and check to see that the leading edge of the iron (the bevel) is parallel to the sole across its entire width.

To retard the iron of a wooden plane, tap gently on the back of the plane and then on the top of the wedge. If the iron needs to be removed and reset, give the plane a sharp tap on the back end.

planes. The variety of species that has been used over the past couple of centuries is mind boggling, and contemporary toolmakers continue that tradition at distinguished companies such as Clark & Williams, White Mountain Toolworks, and Knight Toolworks, among others. In those and other shops, superior craftsmen still use beech for bodies, but they also have access to a host of exotic species such as Ipe, padouk, purpleheart and Goncavo alves (also known as tigerwood, or kingwood). For the most part, though, kiln dried European beech is the most popular species used in wooden-bodied planes.

Furniture builders like wooden planes because the soles, being constantly burnished by the wood they're working, build up a patina rather quickly.

Knight Toolworks

Today, infill planes are collected more for the fine work that goes into making them than any innate ability to deliver a better cut. As with most aspects of planes, certain enthusiasts would argue the point.

How to Adjust a Wooden Plane

To adjust the iron in a wooden plane, it's a good idea to use a wooden, plastic or rawhide mallet. A standard shop hammer is a bit too severe, but specialty hammers are available from several companies including Chester Toolworks. Lay two sheets of printer paper, one on top of the other, on a flat surface such as the cast iron top of a table saw. These are to protect a newly sharpened edge. Place the stock (body) on the paper, and then gently place the iron in the stock. Place the wedge in the stock, and tap it home with one gentle tap of the mallet. Turn the

Knight Toolworks

The maker usually sets the throat opening on an infill plane for a thin shaving, and it's not easily adjusted. These planes are heavy, with very thick irons that help prevent chatter.

plane over, and check that the iron is projecting evenly across the width of the sole. If it leans one way or the other, lightly tap the edge of the iron close to the top, to straighten it. At this point, take a pass on the edge of a board to see how it cuts. If you need to take a smaller cut, tap once gently on the back of the plane, and then once gently on the top of the wedge. Test again. If the iron needs to be removed and reset, give the plane one sharp tap on the back end to loosen the wedge.

Infill Planes

An infill plane is made by dovetailing a metal sole to metal sides, and filling in the void(s) between the sides with hardwood. Originally the best-known names in this genre were Thomas Norris of London and Stewart Spiers of Scotland, although there are now numerous talented craftsmen on both sides of the Atlantic who are both duplicating and improving on the original design. These new planes can cost as much as several thousand dollars each, reflecting the amount of hand work that goes into their manufacture.

Norris invented an adjustment mechanism around the end of World War I that gave him an edge in the market, but both companies produced magnificent planes (although some of the later Spiers are not quite as admirable as the earlier ones).

Thomas Norris & Son began production somewhere between 1860 and 1880 (there is confusion and debate, some of it acerbic, about the actual start date), and continued to produce superior products until about 1940. These planes, executed in iron, steel and brass with rosewood and ebony infills, were quite expensive and worth every penny.

The body of an infill plane is made by first creating dovetails along both edges of the sole, and then milling matching pins along the bottom edges of the steel sides. Sometimes, two contrasting metals (for example, brass or bronze and steel) are used, for both aesthetic and practical reasons. The tails can actually be sloped in both planes (unlike a wooden dovetail), because the edges of malleable metal plates can be bent and shaped with a peen (a special hammer). This locks the parts together, and the joints are then ground and lapped for a perfectly smooth finish.

Some of the restrictions and benefits of infill planes include the fact that the throat is generally not adjustable, and is usually set for a very thin shaving; they are heavy (sometimes very heavy), which adds a degree of control; the irons are often thick and inflexible, to avert chatter; and the set of the iron (the angle at which it lies in the body) is usually quite steep, which of course works best with a heavy body.

While an infill plane is beautiful, one of the new bench planes from companies such as Lie-Nielsen, Clifton or Veritas will equal and usually exceed their performance, and do so at a fraction of the cost. However, a handmade infill plane is a very special tool, worthy of collection and reverence, and an absolute joy to use. Among the better modern manufacturers are Karl Holtey, Sauer & Steiner Toolworks, Steve Knight, Wayne Anderson, Malcolm Macpherson, Bill Carter, C. R. Miller Planes, and Phil Ashby.

In a conversation with Steve Knight of Knight Toolworks in Portland, Oregon, the toolmaker commented on the performance of the planes that he builds. "All well-tuned metal planes work fine on normal woods, but when you start getting grain changes and curl and such, then an infill starts to take over. I have noticed that one of my infills, with an iron bedded at the same angle as a wood bodied plane, will handle grain changes better. I believe this is due to the mass of the plane, the way it absorbs vibration, and the superior bedding of the iron. But, beyond performance, I have also discovered that people buy infills for the coolness factor. What sets an infill apart, I think, is a combination of accuracy, stability and a great way to bed the iron and absorb vibration. The more soundly the iron is bedded, the better the plane can handle crazy grain."

Transitional Planes

Also known as transition planes, these hybrids spanned the void between early wooden-bodied planes and the modern metal body. Their heyday was from about 1875 to 1890, although some manufacturers made them as late at the period between the Wars. The sole on a transitional plane is generally a large, thick block of hardwood (usually beech or maple), while everything else except the tote is metal (usually cast iron). One advantage to this is that the carpenter or cabinetmaker could trim, shape, repair or even replace the base, which wasn't so easy with metal planes. Craftsmen who were used to making their own planes could save time by buying what were actually quite affordable tools in their day.

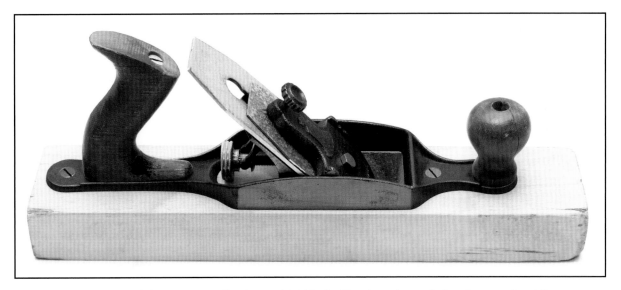

The bulk of a transitional plane is generally a large, thick block of hardwood, usually beech or maple, while everything else except the tote is metal. After removing the blade, the sole can be flattened on a jointer.

History of Hand Planes
Chaplin

King of the hardware stores in New York, the Tower & Lyon company had their own line of hand planes during the 1880s that were produced under patents owned by O.R. Chaplin. The line was an effort by the hardware giant to compete with Stanley Rule & Level in next-door Connecticut, and while they sold well enough, the demand simply wasn't there to sustain the effort. The jacks and jointers had flat soles, and the smoothers were offered with optional corrugated bottoms at the same price as flat soles.

What set Tower & Lyon tools apart (both the Chaplin line and a less well-engineered line called the Challenge) was their handles. Choices on the Chaplin planes included nickel-coated iron totes, or a checkered India rubber. The cheaper Challenge planes had a curved wooden tote that looked like a limp bratwurst, and worked about as well.

The Chaplin tools were extremely similar to Leonard Bailey's original planes, although Tower & Lyon named them differently. Their small smoother was the No. 202, and the large jointer was the No. 211. Prices at the height of production in 1886 ranged from $3 for a smoother to $6.75 for a jointer, and their No. 20 and 30 block planes (Japanned and nickel-plated respectively) were a bargain at $1.40 and $1.65.

Peter McBride / petermcbride.com

Stanley produced a full line of transitional bench planes including No. 21, 22, 23 and 24 smoothers; No. 25 block; No. 26, 27 and 27½ jack; No. 28 and 29 fore; and five jointers, the No. 30, 31, 32, 33 and 34. Later, the company added No. 35 and 36 coffin-shaped smoothers, and the No. 37 jenny, a light and shorter version of a jack. On models made before 1912, the cast iron frame is screwed to the beech body. After that date, machine screws and bushings are used.

Other manufacturers (primarily in New England but also makers such as the Ohio Tool Company, Auburn Metallic in New York, Sargent, Union, Birmingham and even Siegley) either copied or independently developed planes similar to the line of Stanley transitionals. For collectors, their short manufacturing life yet relatively widespread distribution means that few models are really valuable (mostly the smallest smoother and block planes).

History of Hand Planes
Clifton

A relative newcomer to the hand planes industry, Clico (Sheffield) Tooling Limited and their Clifton line of planes bear mentioning. The company began making specialty planes for cabinetmakers and furniture builders in 1985. The line includes shoulder/rabbet planes, shaves, scrapers and, of course, bench planes. Aesthetically pleasing, they receive an almost universal thumbs-up from serious woodworkers for quality control and design. The factory uses a mix of traditional and state-of-the-art technologies, including both hand forging and laser machining. Their bench planes are equipped with heavy forged irons, and the tools are based on the classic Stanley Bedrock line. Clifton's shoulder planes have an interesting pedigree: They are essentially reincarnations of the great Edward Preston & Sons planes, having come to Clico via the Record Company, which bought them in 1934.

Erik Edstrom / traditionalwoodworker.com

Many transitional planes bear the image of the Liberty Bell and the date '76, commemorating the nation's centenary. Others, the early Stanleys, show an eagle. Massachusetts author Roger Smith (**RogerKSmith.com**) has written two definitive books on these planes.

Transitional planes are a little difficult to use. Despite their bulk, they lack mass and weight, so they skim across a surface. Once a patina has been established on the sole through use, they glide a little better. However, they also wear very quickly, and often list to one side like a ship taking on water. Consequently, many transitionals have had a layer of harder wood added to the bottom of the sole by their owners. Some have even had metal added to areas of high wear on the soles, while others have had apple wood or a similar dense species inset to close the throat, an effort to produce more controlled cuts and lighter shavings.

Chapter 6
How to Sharpen a Bench Plane Iron

The most important part of a plane is the leading edge of the iron (blade). If the iron isn't sharp, the plane won't work. Sharpening a plane iron is a three-step process. The back (unbeveled) face of the iron must be made flat; then the bevel must be established by grinding; and finally, the bevel must be sharpened by honing.

In use, an iron generates heat. Heat, combined with changes in ambient temperature over the years, the effects of gravity, the molecular make-up of the steel, misuse, rust and other stress factors can leave an iron less than perfectly flat. Sometimes an old burr remains on the leading edge, or an impact has deformed the edge. Whatever the reason, the backs of old and even brand new irons usually need to be flattened prior to sharpening. The process employed to flatten the back is called lapping. On bench plane irons, only the half-inch or so closest to the cutting edge needs to be lapped. The reasoning here is that flattening the entire back of the iron will not affect the leading edge's ability to cut. That's a good thing, because it saves a lot of work. Strictly speaking, nothing beyond the actual bevel needs to be flat, but it's impractical to work only that much of the iron, so we opt for flattening the leading half-inch or so.

The best way to lap the back of an iron is to drag out the bench stones. It can be done on lapping plates, too (plate glass or flat granite with various grits of wet/dry sandpaper attached to them), but bench stones are faster and deliver better results. Another viable

Stanley Tool Works

option is to use a slow, wet horizontal wheel. This is a fine-grit grinding wheel that lies flat, so the side is used to sharpen, rather than the narrow edge. Unfortunately, geometry works against us here. A spot located on the outside edge of a horizontal 8" diameter wheel travels about 25" during every revolution of the wheel. A spot located 3" from the center of the wheel (that is, along an arc describing a 6" diameter) travels just under 19". So, in the same amount of time that the outside edge of the wheel makes one complete revolution, this inside spot is traveling at about ¾ the speed. If a 2" wide plane iron is being sharpened on a horizontal wheel and it

A slow wet grinder is a great way to sharpen a plane iron, but horizontal grinders use the side of the stone so they grind unevenly. (In a revolution, the edge has to travel farther than any point closer in.)

is held radially (that is, along an imaginary straight line between the center of the wheel and the perimeter), the outside corner of the cutting edge is being ground 25% more than the inside edge. The inside edge will generate more heat, but that's pretty negligible on a slow-turning, water-cooled wheel. The ideal solution here is to hold the iron at a 90° angle to the radius, which is impractical and doesn't take any stress factors into account. So, most of us end up guessing on a compromise angle and applying more pressure to the trailing edge, which pretty much defeats the purpose of the tool rest.

To use bench stones, charge your water stones by immersing them fully in water for at least half an hour—longer if there are any bubbles still rising. Using distilled or filtered water, such as is found in potable bottles bought at the store, is a good idea. City or even well water tends to have a lot of impurities, and the chemicals added to kill bacteria, add fluorides, boost salines

(for water softening), and otherwise treat the water may or may not be harmful to stones. Most water stones are manmade, but some older ones and many of the more expensive Japanese stones are all natural, and the bonding in these sedimentary rocks can be delicate.

During use, add generous amounts of the appropriate lubricant. For

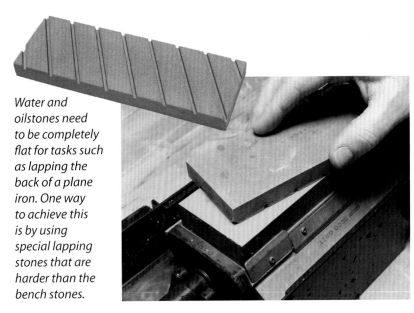

Water and oilstones need to be completely flat for tasks such as lapping the back of a plane iron. One way to achieve this is by using special lapping stones that are harder than the bench stones.

There's no need to flatten the entire back of a plane iron. Work only the leading ½" or so, unless it is pitted so badly that it won't lie flat on the frog without chattering.

water and diamond stones, this is bottled water. For oilstones, it's a light kerosene or a dedicated sharpening fluid. The liquid is not simply a cleaning agent. It also allows small, discarded particles of the sharpening stone to be gathered in an abrasive slurry that the abrasives industry calls a swarf. This swarf speeds up the grinding or honing process.

Water and oilstones need to be checked for flatness before they are used to lap the backs of plane irons. Undulations can be seen when a steel straightedge is held against the top of the stone, with a background of bright light. Check both diagonals, and then check across the stone with a square. If there is incongruity, use a special leveling stone (actually called a lapping stone) or a diamond stone to flatten the water or oilstones. Diamond stones are absolutely flat because they are actually steel plates with a coating of nickel into which the diamond particles are embedded. They don't wear unevenly.

The primary bevel on a plane iron is generally ground to 25°, and a small 2° secondary bevel (often called a micro-bevel) is honed on its edge. The secondary bevel is all that needs to be touched up during use.

Begin lapping with the most aggressive stone and work down through the grits to the finest available. A good selection of water stones is 1000, 4000 and 8000. Clean the area and iron each time you change grits, as residue from a coarser grit can contaminate a finer stone and cause scratches. Using lots of water, hold the iron flat on the surface so that about ½" of iron rests on the stone. Slide the iron back and forth, checking visually after each dozen or so strokes. The iron should have the same scratch pattern across its full width when it has been lapped enough on each stone. Skewing the iron a couple of degrees in alternating directions as each stone is used leaves a more visible scratch pattern. (That is, angle the iron two or three degrees to the right on the coarsest stone, a couple of degrees to the left on the medium stone, and then back to the right on the finest stone.)

An 8" soft friable stone traveling slowly (about 800 RPM) is a great choice for a grindstone. This larger diameter has 33% more surface than a 6" wheel, producing less heat and delivering a shallower hollow grind.

With the back of the iron perfectly flat, it's time to address the front beveled edge. Most bench plane irons actually have two bevels, a large primary one and a small secondary one. The larger bevel is usually ground at 25°, and the secondary adds another couple of degrees so it cuts at 27° or 28°. However, many planes don't follow this rule. Scrapers, for example, are generally ground at 45°. Check with the individual plane manufacturer on low- and high-angle planes, bevel-up planes and all specialty planes where the iron doesn't rest bevel down in the body at approximately 45°.

If the manufacturer doesn't have contact information or a Web site available, do a search for the specific plane on the Internet and look for sharpening instructions. Blogs and online discussion groups, forums and message boards are great resources for practical information on the subject.

Grind the primary bevel on a motorized stone, or use coarse diamond bench stones. Oilstones and water stones simply take too long. A slow (1000 RPM or thereabouts) 8" diameter stone is the best choice. The slow speed helps mitigate heat buildup, and the larger diameter produces less of a hollow grind than a six-inch wheel. Stones are either direct drive (attached to an arbor on the motor), so they travel at whatever speed the motor is rated, or indirect (pulley) driven. To determine the speed of a pulley drive, divide the diameter of the motor pulley by the diameter of the grinder pulley and then multiply the result by the motor's RPM rating. For example, a 1725 RPM motor set up with a 2.5" diameter pulley that is linked to a grindstone arbor equipped with a 6" diameter pulley will turn the stone at the ideal speed of 719 RPM. A stone spinning at 3450 RPM (the speed of most inexpensive bench grinders) is far too fast for sharpening tool steel. The ideal stone is a fine-grit, soft, friable white wheel.

The grinder should have a tool-rest set

Charge a hard white cotton buffing wheel with an abrasive such as Flexcut's Gold Polishing Compound. This is used to remove the wire burr created on the cutting edge by the grindstone.

to deliver a 25° bevel. Keep the iron moving from side to side across the stone at all times to create an even bevel and avoid heat buildup. Grind for a few seconds, and then dip the iron in cool water to dissipate any heat. If an iron turns blue at the tip, it is essentially ruined. By the time it turns visibly blue, it has already run through a complete spectrum of less visible colors as heat has gradually built up along the leading edge and worked up the iron, drawing the temper from it. This means that the iron is now too brittle to hold an edge. Two seconds on the stone and then a quick quenching in water is a sensible sequence. Honing won't usually repair an error in grinding (unless one hones for several hours), so care must be taken to achieve an even, straight grind with no nicks.

To keep track of the way a stone is grinding a bevel, mark the steel with a permanent marker or machinist's blue dye. As the edge is dressed, the ink is removed and low spots easily seen.

Once ground, the secondary bevel can be established by honing on bench stones. Set a honing guide to 27° and work down through the grits to the finest stone available, using lots of lubricant. Don't attempt to hone without a jig, as consistency is paramount here. Without a jig, one essentially ends up honing several differently angled bevels at the same time. (The one exception here is when a woodworker uses Shapton ceramic stones and faithfully follows Harrelson Stanley's instruction on the company's DVD.)

When changing from one grit to the next, briefly pass the iron across a charged cotton buffing wheel, to remove the wire burr created on the stone.

History of Hand Planes
Henry Cope

In the early 1880s, a patternmaker for Detroit Stove Works invented the first router plane. It was patented in March of 1884, and Cope sold the design to Stanley Rule and Level Company later that year. Within months, Stanley produced and sold the new plane as the No. 71 (which was a bit bigger than Cope's original). An 1887 Stanley ad for this remarkably useful and extremely popular tool read that it was "perfectly adapted to smooth the bottom of grooves, panels, or all depressions below the general surface of any woodwork." Generations of woodworkers have thanked Mr. Cope.

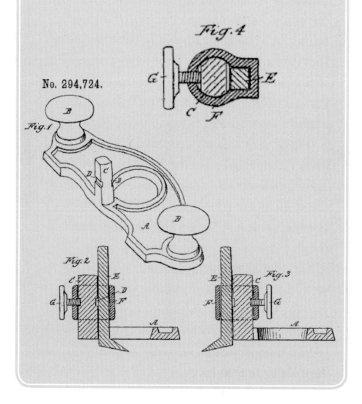

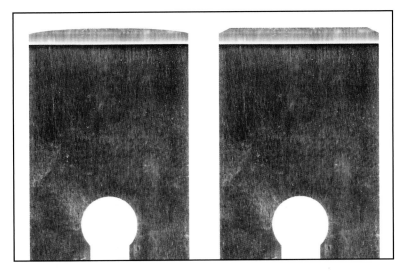

To prevent sharp corners from digging into the wood, crown the edge of a smoother iron with a slow, gentle arc, or hone a curve or chamfer (shown) on the last ¼" or so at either end of the cutting edge.

It's a good idea to mark the bevel black with a permanent marker, as this makes it very easy to see exactly where the stones are abrading the steel. Another alternative is to use machinist's blue dye, made by Starret and available from Highland Woodworking and other suppliers. According to the Highland catalog, "this opaque, fast-drying dye will give you the reference surface you need. Find out exactly where parts make contact (and where they don't)." It can be removed using alcohol or lacquer thinner, but by the time the last stone has done its work, the dye will have disappeared and the bevel will be mirror smooth and bright.

Most professionals go one step further on their smoothing and block plane irons by crowning the edge. This means that they will either establish a slow, very gentle curve across the entire width of the iron, or else they will touch up the last ¼" or so at either edge, and then hone it back at a very slight angle. The idea here is to stop the sharp outside corners of these field planes (where the work is wider than the iron, as opposed to jointer planes where the wood is narrower than the iron) from digging into the surface of the work and leaving scratches or mill marks. It takes only a few seconds to ease the outer edge on the last couple of passes across the finest stone. This is a very subtle process. Simply leaning the jig very slightly to each side will accomplish your goal. This is achieved by transferring the pressure first to one side and then to the other. By the way, crowning can be tricky on a Tormek® sharpening system—I've found that bench stones work better. This is honestly the only time that I would

A scrub plane's dramatic arc along the cutting edge enables it to remove large amounts of wood in each pass. The arc is ground by swiveling the iron from side to side in a gentle, regular motion.

recommend bench stones over the impressive Tormek system.

On scrub planes, which have a very severe crown designed to hog out lots of material quickly (such as on chair seats), the bevel is established on the grinder by swiveling the iron from side to side in a gentle, well-paced motion that creates an even arc across the cutting edge. It actually works best to hone such an edge on a 1"x 42" belt sander (the 30" version seems to build up heat too quickly), using special honing belts available from Klingspor, while setting the tool rest table at 27°.

After honing, it's very important to set the iron in the plane so that it is absolutely parallel with the sole. If it is locked in place at even a very slight angle, it will leave tracks on one side of the cut.

During the course of honing, a small burr will build up on the back of the iron. This can actually be felt with fingertips. After the last pass on the bevel, turn the iron over and quickly lap the back on the finest stone to remove any wire edge left by the honing. Another option here is to use a charged, firm cotton buffing wheel or polish the back with a leather strop, but the stone usually does a pretty good job.

While working the bevel, some people stop and lap the back of the iron on each of the grits before changing to the next finest stone, but that's usually not necessary. Purists, hold your peace.

History of Hand Planes
Karl Hotley

For the past two decades, Scotland's Karl Holtey has been one of the world's premier custom plane makers. Expanding on the work of Spiers, Mathieson and Norris, he is perhaps the leading authority on the construction of British style infill planes. Hotley, who began his working life as a cabinetmaker, works alone in a well-equipped tool room in Lairg, a village of about 700 people on the shores of a lake in the most northern reaches of the Scottish Highlands. Aside from his breathtakingly beautiful (and not inexpensive) planes, Hotley has begun to change the way small toolmakers look at plane irons. His S53 Blades are "made from powder metallurgical steel, which has basically the same characteristics as the A2. Tests have shown that the edge will last several times longer than the A2 blades, saving even more down time. The blades are treated in a vacuum furnace to a high temperature to achieve a hardness of HRC64. They are also triple tempered and cryogenically treated."

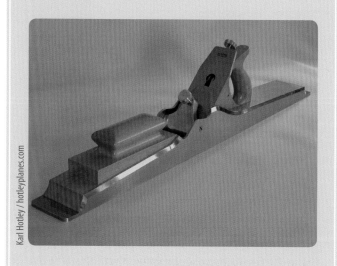

Karl Hotley / hotleyplanes.com

Chapter 7

How to Tune a Bench Plane

Parts of a Plane

While sharpening an iron (blade) is definitely the most important aspect of making a plane work well, a complete plane tune-up delivers truly inspiring results. A well-tuned plane glides across the work with almost no resistance, creating paper-thin shavings. Even brand new planes often need to be tuned up, as many of them are assembled and packaged by people who aren't woodworkers, or the company saves a little time and money by allowing us the privilege of doing it ourselves. The process requires some familiarity with various parts

of a typical bench plane, and an awareness of the quirky names that have evolved for these parts.

On traditional wooden planes, the body was typically called the stock, and some woodworkers still use that term even when discussing cast iron planes. However, most people today just call it the body. The bottom of the body is the sole. At the rear of the plane is the handle, or tote. At the front is a knob that helps guide the tool, and also applies downward pressure.

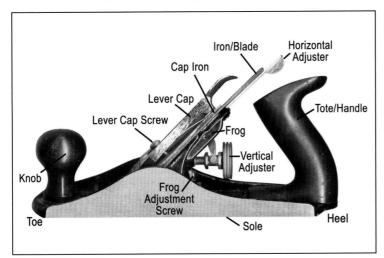

Most cast iron bench planes are remarkably similar in construction to the Stanley Bailey No. 4 shown here, with the main differences being the length of their soles and the width of the irons.

In the middle of the plane, a somewhat complicated assembly holds the iron at the correct angle and allows for adjustment of the iron up and down and the tilt from side to side. The largest part of this assembly is a cast iron triangle called the frog. The frog is attached to the body with two machine screws. For most bench planes, the frog holds the iron at about 45°. This is known as the bedding angle. On low-angle planes (used on end grain), the front of the frog is sloped at about 12° (it varies a bit with different manufacturers). The frogs on high angle planes (used for difficult grain) generally have a front slope of 47° to 55°. A small piece of U-shaped metal is attached upside-down to the back of the frog, and this sits on the frog adjustment screw . This screw is used to move the frog back and forth, which has the effect of opening or closing the throat (mouth) of the plane. The throat is the rectangular-shaped hole in the sole of the plane, where the blade sticks through. When the depth of cut is minimal (for a thin shaving), the throat should be closed, perhaps no more than ¹⁄₁₆" away from the iron. When thick shavings are required to remove lots of wood in a hurry, the cut is deeper and the throat should be wide open. Most of the time, the opening for the throat is somewhere between these extremes.

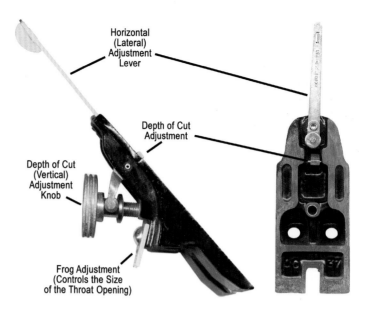

Despite the marketing claims, a Bailey frog doesn't really look like a real frog. Virtually unchanged over the past one hundred years, it holds the iron at the correct angle, and can be moved forward to close the throat.

A small steel plate with two screws in it controls the size of the throat. The top screw secures the plate to the frog, and the bottom screw adjusts the frog back and forth (two locking screws above must be loose).

The lever cap is a piece of steel (often chromed and bearing the maker's name or logo) with a toggle clamp built into it. The handle of this clamp is called the lever, hence the name lever cap. The plane's iron is sandwiched between the frog and the lever cap, and the lever then allows the user to remove the iron quickly for sharpening—and replace it quickly, too. A large machine screw called the lever cap screw extends through holes in the lever cap and the iron, and this screw is then threaded into the sloped face of the frog.

The irons in Japanese planes are quite thick. Traditionally, Western wooden planes had thick irons, too. But when cast iron planes came along, the iron was now held in place with a

History of Hand Planes
Keen Kutter

While not significant in the development of hand planes, the name Keen Kutter is relatively important in the marketing of them. The planes were sold by the Simmons Hardware Company, which was established in either 1870 or 1874, depending on the source one trusts. The company was located in St. Louis, Missouri, which was a gateway to the developing Western states. Simmons eventually developed more than eight hundred workshop and household products under the Keen Kutter name. The hand planes were actually a reincarnation of earlier Bedrock models, and the first batch were made by the Ohio Tool Company in 1907. After that, Stanley took over. Simmons eventually became Val-Test Distributors Buying Group, which buys and sells hardware and other items on a wholesale basis.

Larry Meeker / Patented-Antiques.com

On top of the frog a cam-action lever applies pressure that locks a steel cap in place, and this lever cap in turn secures the iron to the frog. When it's time to sharpen, the cam is simply raised to release the iron.

A cap iron is a piece of steel attached to the iron that looks a bit like a blade, but instead of a cutting bevel it has a rounded leading edge that breaks chips and allows them to curl up through the throat.

metal screw rather than a wooden wedge, and it seemed to Stanley's engineers that it would be fully supported by the sloped front face of the frog. So, logic said that the iron could afford to be a bit thinner, and hence less expensive to make. However, it didn't take woodworkers long to realize that thin irons under pressure still flexed a little, even in a cast iron body. The result was chatter, and the manufacturer's response was to add a second layer to the blade, which came to be known as the cap iron. The cap iron was (and is) held tightly to the iron with a short, wide screw. Made of plate steel, the cap iron serves two purposes. Not only does it reinforce the iron and eliminate flexing, it also provides a way to break shavings so they curl up and move out of the way of subsequent waste. So, the leading edge of the cap iron is slightly curled, and this curl is called a chipbreaker.

Let's take a break from nomenclature for a while, and work through the actual tune-up.

Steps in a Tune-Up

The first step in making a plane work more efficiently is to clean up any rust, corrosion, paint or other finish residue on the sides and sole of the body. Spray a light coat of penetrating solvent on these surfaces, and then work them with #0000 steel wool. Wipe off the oil and debris with a clean rag.

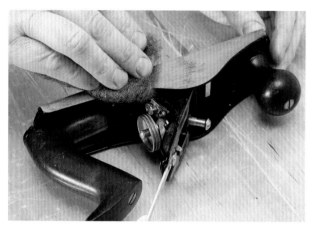

The first step in restoring or tuning a plane is to remove resins, dirt and corrosion. Apply a light coat of penetrating solvent onto the sides and sole of the body and then work them with #0000 steel wool.

Next, make the sole perfectly flat. A local machine shop can do this, and it is surprisingly inexpensive to have done. But it only takes a few minutes to do it in the woodshop, and it's both fun and rewarding. This job is variously known as dressing, lapping or even fettering. Many of the more obscure names in the hand tool world originally described tasks that were performed by 17th and 18th century English carriage builders, and there's an argument that fettering once described the way in which horses hooves were floated to flatten them for shoes. In old English, the word "feter" meant foot, so fettering perhaps has something to do with fetlocks. In later centuries, fettering was the word used to describe the practice of applying steel manacles to a prisoner's feet. (Now, there's something that would certainly flatten your soul...)

The easiest way to flatten a bench plane's sole is with wet/dry silicon carbide sandpaper. Use a spray adhesive to secure the paper to a perfectly flat surface. Some

Before lapping the sole to flatten it, mark it with a snaking line drawn with a permanent marker. As the abrasives work, this line will identify high and low spots. When it's gone, the sole is flat.

woodworkers use only mineral spirits for this, trusting that the liquid will hold the paper in place, and it usually does. Options for the substrate include plate glass, the polished (top) face of a granite tile, or even the cast iron wing of an old table saw. Begin with 120-grit paper if the sole is badly pitted or corroded, but 220-grit will generally do the trick. Leave the blade in the plane so that the body remains under normal stress, but retard the iron so that none of it is exposed. Before sanding, hold the plane up before daylight or a lamp, and check the flatness of the sole with a straightedge. This will give you a general idea of what to expect in terms of the amount of material that needs to be removed. Make marks on the sole with a permanent marker or machinist's ink so that you can keep track of high and low spots as you work. An "S" pattern works well. Douse the paper lightly with a spray bottle of water to lubricate it, and continue to spray moisture periodically as you flatten the sole. Work down through the grits from 220 to 320, then 400 and 600. When all of the marks have been abraded, the sole is flat.

Gently break the edges of the sole with 320-grit sandpaper after lapping—this removes any small burr left by the sandpaper, or indeed the manufacturer. Check with a square to make sure that the sides are at true 90° angles to the sole. If not, they may have to be machined at a metalworking shop. This rarely happens, and then only when the plane has been dropped. Abuse is generally not an issue, as woodworkers are far too cultured to ever vent their frustrations on a helpless tool.

Using water as a lubricant, lap the sole down through the grits from 220 to 600. It's important to leave the iron in the plane so that the body is under normal stress. Retard the cutting edge into the body, to avoid sanding it.

The chipbreaker is the leading edge of the cap iron. Dress the bottom face while holding it at an angle off the side of a bench stone (shown), and then buff the top with a hard cotton wheel charged with buffing compound.

The next step is to touch up the chipbreaker. This is the leading edge of the cap iron, and it needs to be absolutely flat along its bottom edge so that it forms a perfect seal with the back of the iron. The mating edges must leave no place for shavings to intrude. The best way to do this is on a series of bench stones, working from coarse to fine. Remove the lever cap, cap iron and iron from the plane, and then work on the chipbreaker. Be careful to remove the absolute minimum amount of material, as removing too much will actually open a gap. Hold the cap iron at a slight downward angle (just a couple of degrees), so that only the very edge of the chipbreaker is being worked.

On block planes, which don't usually have a cap iron, it's a good idea to flatten the leading edge of the lever cap. Sometimes the factory leaves a few small burrs under there, and they can allow the iron to chatter.

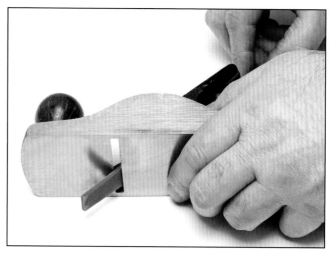

Next, remove the frog from the body by withdrawing the two machine screws that hold it in place. Clean the cavity below the frog, and the frog itself, using a toothbrush dipped in water. Thoroughly dry these metal parts to avoid corrosion. With the frog out of the way, there is good access to the throat. Use a fine file to remove any slight burrs along its edges that were left by the factory during either milling or the application of Japanning. Japanning is the traditional black finish used on planes, and it's either a hard shiny varnish or paint, depending on where and when it was done.

Sometimes a casting from the factory leaves small indentations, build-ups, or uneven edges on the throat of a plane. These can be quickly removed by feeding a fine file down through the blade opening.

On many planes, the throat opening is not adjusted by moving the frog but by sliding the portion of the sole that lies in front of the throat. This is done by loosening the knob on top of the plane. During a tune-up, remove the knob entirely and then remove the adjustable portion of the sole. File any burrs that you find in the ways (the dovetailed

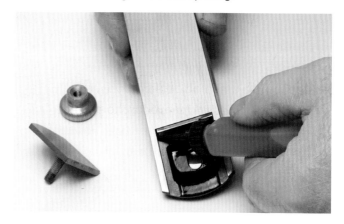

On planes where the throat is adjusted by sliding a plate in the sole back and forth, it helps if the ways (guides) for the plate are cleaned out and oiled occasionally. Use a thin lubricant such as sewing machine oil.

channels that allow this part to slide), and then remove any debris before applying a thin coat of light machine oil on the ways. Reinstall the adjustable sole and secure it with the knob. At this time you can also oil the vertical adjustment screw mechanism behind the frog, which controls the depth of cut. Be careful to oil only the adjuster itself—not the threads on the screw.

Reassemble the Plane

With all of the parts cleaned and touched up, it's time to put the plane back together. Install the frog with its two screws, but don't fully secure them just yet. Leave the screws snug, but not tight. If you haven't done so already, sharpen the iron. (There are full instructions in the previous chapter.) Attach the cap iron to the iron, leaving the chipbreaker 1/16" shy of the leading edge of the iron. Tighten the screw securely, and then place the iron on the frog. Install the lever cap and adjust the frog so that the throat is where it needs to be. Remove the lever cap, cap iron

History of Hand Planes
Lee Valley and Veritas

Founded in 1978, Lee Valley is a family-owned business whose manufacturing arm, Veritas® Tools Inc., has earned a reputation as a leading maker and designer of hand planes. Based in Ottawa, the company operates several retail stores across Canada, and has a large presence in the U.S. market via catalog and reseller sales. The factory employs about 140 people. A willingness to listen to woodworkers and incorporate their ideas in plane designs has been part of the development strategy since the company's inception. Over the years, Veritas has focused on better adjustment and feed mechanisms, structural innovations to prevent blade vibration, and blades that offer a choice of bevels and metallurgical properties. The planes are "manufactured from fully stress-relieved ductile cast iron, which maintains its dimensions after machining and takes harder knocks without cracking." In its thirty-year history, the company has created a comprehensive line of bench, block and specialty planes.

Lee Valley & Veritas

Reassemble the plane and set the iron so that it takes the thinnest of cuts. Shavings should be ribbon-like and so thin that they are nearly transparent. A cut that's too aggressive leads to chatter, and frustration.

and iron, and fully tighten the two screws used to secure the frog. Then replace the iron, cap iron and lever cap. Adjust the lever so that it snaps tight securely, but can still be opened relatively easily.

Adjusting the depth of cut is next—that is, the amount of the iron that protrudes through the sole. Less is better here. Most people who are learning how to use a hand plane tend to leave far too much of the iron exposed. When the iron is properly adjusted, it will remove the high spots in its first couple of passes and sometimes doesn't begin to deliver long, thin shavings until the third or fourth pass. So, patience is necessary. Check the lateral adjustment so that the iron is perfectly parallel to the sole. Apply a coat of paste wax (beeswax or paraffin) to the sole, and the job is done. Once tuned, a plane usually lasts a long time before it needs the full treatment again.

One last note: when storing freshly tuned planes, lay them on their sides or place a pencil under one end, to elevate the body and protect the cutting edge.

Chapter 8
How to Flatten a Board

Let's first look at why one would use a hand plane to flatten a board, and then we'll see how to do it. There are two practical occasions when a hand plane is a great choice for this task. The first is when a board is too wide for the jointer, or a jointer isn't available. The second is when several boards have been edge glued to make a panel, and the joints need to be dressed.

Beyond the practical, there are also aesthetic reasons to flatten stock with a hand plane. The mere act of working the board by hand requires that a woodworker pay great attention to the grain direction, color and defects. This means that he or she is far more likely to choose materials wisely, and to match them well. Such attention to detail brings cohesiveness to a project, a look of intent rather than random choice.

Parts flow together visually, and the whole seems well balanced in terms of color and texture.

There is, too, an element of reflection to a hand planed panel. If done well, it is crisp and flat, but still has some depth to it, and a raking light will almost imperceptibly dance across the undulations left by the iron. (I've been told that this effect can be enhanced by the presence of twelve-year-old Scotch.)

While it would be romantic to adopt a purist attitude and eschew power tools completely, for most of us who have limited time in the shop, it just isn't very practical. A jointer can deliver a flat face on a board in a few seconds, while using a series of planes takes considerably longer. (See sidebar on page 59.) But the jointer in most home shops is restricted to a face cut that is only 6" wide. If you need a wider board, it's time to reach for a smoothing plane.

Using Machines to Flatten Stock

An electric jointer is used to flatten one face of a board. When fed into a thickness planer, it mills the second face parallel to the first. The pros say that a jointer makes a board flat but not parallel, while a planer makes a board parallel but not flat. In other words, if a board with a slight bow is fed into a planer, it will come out the other end with its faces clean and totally parallel to each other, but it will still be bowed. It should first have been passed across a jointer. The following is a very brief discussion on using the jointer and planer to create flat, straight stock. It covers the most common defects that can be fixed on these machines. Of course, the same work can be done with hand planes and the experience will be quieter, far less dusty, and eminently more satisfying and Zen-like. But, unfortunately, it will take longer.

Bow:

A bowed board is one that is curved from one end to the other. When laid on one face with the bow up, it forms a low bridge. If the bow isn't too severe, it can be fixed on a jointer. Begin by scribbling a long, weaving pencil line across the inside face (think of an archer's bow: the inside is the face closest to the archer).

On the first pass, feed the board across the jointer with the arch up until the cutters no longer make contact (it stops making noise), and lift the board off the jointer. Then reverse the board end-for-end and, with the arch still oriented up, repeat the process on the other end. Trimming the ends in this manner will reduce the amount of work that the jointer must do on subsequent passes. On the third pass, feed the entire board across the jointer, and continue making full passes until the pencil lines disappear. The bottom face of the board is now flat, and the top face can now be made parallel to it (and, of course, flat) by feeding the board through a thickness planer.

The bow is too severe for this solution if, after flattening the top in the planer, it will be too thin for its intended purpose. This can be determined before going to the jointer by standing the board on one edge and laying a long straightedge on the other edge, to preview the results of jointing. If it will be too thin, crosscutting the board into two shorter lengths can reduce the amount of bow.

Crook:

A crooked board is one that is relatively flat, but the sides are curved. Feed one edge across the jointer with the middle of the curve facing up. If the curve is down, the board will rock from end to end on the jointer bed. If the crook is pretty severe, use a jackplane to knock down the points (that is, just work the ends of the bottom edge so that the entire edge is closer to being straight), before running it across the jointer. A No. 7 or No. 8 bench plane will also straighten the edge once the points have been knocked down, and the second edge can then be straightened on a table saw.

A straight-lining jig for the table saw is another option. This is a piece of plywood to which the crooked board is attached with clamps. The board extends past one edge of the plywood, and the other edge of the plywood rides against the table saw's fence. This makes it safe to run a crooked board through the table saw, to render the cantilevered edge straight.

A note of caution here: Crooked boards, even after straightening, often have tension built up inside them. When they are fed through a table saw, the board remembers how it once was and tries to revert to that shape. This can cause the kerf (the path left by the blade) to close quickly as it emerges from the saw, and pinch the back end of the blade. On saws that are not equipped with a riving knife or a decent splitter (see the MJ Splitter on MicroJig.com's Web site), this will result in violent kickback. Keep a close eye on the kerf and, if it begins to close, stop the saw immediately and hold the board firmly in place until the blade stops spinning.

Cup:

This is a warp across the width of a board. The edges have curled up, and the middle has dropped. Running this board across the jointer several times with the high point (the convex edge) facing up will deliver a flat bottom face, and the top can then be dressed and rendered parallel by a thickness planer. If the board is quite wide and the cup severe, it can first be ripped on the table saw (with the cup down and the "horns" up), as long as one edge is straight. After flattening, the two halves can be edge glued back together after the edges have been jointed.

Twist:

This is a board that is warped across its diagonals. That is, it will rest on diagonally opposite corners when laid on one face. Most often, the best solution here is to call a friend who owns a wood-burning stove. The board can also be crosscut several times to create useful shorter boards that can then be passed across the jointer with their bows up, and completed on the thickness planer with the jointed faces down. Twisted boards have usually air-dried without sufficient weight on them.

Getting Ready

One interesting aspect of bench planes is that we use the longest and largest ones to joint the narrow edges of boards, and the shortest ones to clean up the wide faces of boards. When planing the face of a board, a long plane rides atop the high spots and leave some of the hollows untouched. So, the sequence to flattening a board is to start with a longer plane and switch to a shorter one as the surface evens out. However, if a board is very distorted and a lot of material needs to be removed from one or two areas, a short scrub plane can preempt the longer plane in the sequence. Scrub planes have a very aggressive set, meaning that a lot of the iron protrudes through the sole, and the leading edge of the iron is radically crowned. This means that the plane takes a deep and dramatic channel-shaped cut. A scrub plane cuts so aggressively that it can be used in the process of hollowing out chair seats. When flattening a board, a scrub plane quickly removes large amounts of wood from high spots on a workpiece, such as the crown on a cupped board.

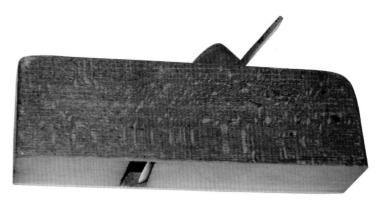

A scrub plane's iron has a dramatically curved cutting edge, which allows it to remove a lot of waste very quickly. A scrub plane is an ideal choice for the initial dressing of cupped and twisted boards.

Keeping boards secure on a workbench can be a problem, as clamps get in the way. In the absence of bench dogs, the work can be wedged between two clamped-on waste boards, using a couple of tapered wedges.

Before using the scrub plane, the first step is to secure the board to a bench. While clamps work well, they do tend to get in the way. Bench dogs work much better. If a bench with dogs isn't available, try clamping slightly thinner scrap near the work (that is, cut-offs that are not as thick as the workpiece), and then use wedges to secure the board.

Prepare for planing by having a long straightedge and a couple of winding sticks on hand. Winding sticks are perfectly straight pieces of wood or steel, about 24" long. You can lay a few of them across a board at intervals, and then sight along the top. As you look across the tops of the winding sticks and line up the top edges (preferably with a light in the distance), they exaggerate tendencies from the norm: If one end of an 8" wide board leans slightly to the left, and the other leans slightly to the right, the winding sticks will multiply this variance so that it is immediately obvious. By extending the visual width of the board by 300% (that is, stretching the 8" to 24"), winding sticks allow the woodworker to pinpoint problem areas when flattening a surface.

Have a caliper on hand, too. Frequently check the thickness of the stock, especially when it begins to approach the desired finished dimension.

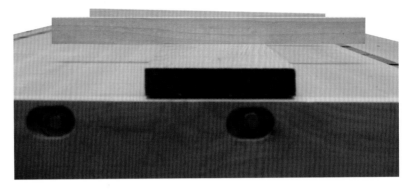

To locate the high spots, winding sticks (straight pieces of wood or steel) are laid across a board. When sighted across they immediately reveal portions of the board that are not perfectly flat.

Choosing Planes

The planes used to flatten a wide face should be sharpened and tuned (see Chapters 6 and 7). A jack or fore plane (No. 5 or No. 6) is the best choice for a long plane, and a No. 3 is ideal for the short, smoothing plane, but a No. 4 will do nicely, too. For this job, I prefer a low-angle Veritas bevel-up smoother over a traditional Stanley Bailey with a 45° bevel-down bedding. The Veritas blade is massive—a full ⅛" thick—and the plane body is quite heavy, lending it even more mass. It's also 10½" long, as opposed to the nominal 9" of a Stanley (although a Bailey No. 4 actually contacts the work along 9¾" of sole). Unfortunately, the Veritas is about four times as expensive. It's worth every penny, but may not be in everyone's budget. For example, my wife has no idea that I own one.

One great option here is to upgrade the Stanley with a heavy Hock iron and cap iron/chipbreaker. Both help reduce chatter. According to Ron Hock, his massive ³⁄₃₂" thick blades "offer a substantial improvement over the inferior chrome-vanadium junk that comes with most new tools. Our high carbon steel blades can be honed easier and sharper. And our cryogenically treated A2 blades will hold an edge longer." He can afford to be so forthright: His products are among the finest ever made. Surprisingly, the cost is quite reasonable. At the beginning of 2009, the BP200 high carbon steel blade for a No. 4 was just $38, and a matching cap iron/chipbreaker (the BK200) was $28. This thicker chipbreaker helps stabilize the blade's cutting edge, reducing vibration and chatter. It measures 3mm. thick (0.118"), which is almost twice as thick as a stock chipbreaker, and they come with a knurled cap screw. See Chapter 13 for more details.

The most common smoother is a Stanley No. 3 or No. 4, but another great choice is a low-angle bevel-up smoother. The Veritas model shown here is a good choice because of its heavy iron and massive body.

The Sequence

If the work being flattened is not a single board, but rather a panel made up of several edge-glued boards, the first step is to remove any hardened, cured glue. This is best done with a scraper rather than a bench plane, as it is tough on a freshly sharpened bevel. A standard paint scraper, adequately sharpened on a strip sander or a grindstone, works well here. When the glue has been removed, switch to a scraper plane, such as a No. 80 or a No. 12, to work out any problems caused by the crude paint scraper.

When we glue up panels in our shop, we apply a strip of blue painter's masking tape about 1/16" shy of each edge being glued. When clamping pressure is applied, the excess glue squeezes out onto this tape. We wait until the glue begins to set and just before it hardens we remove the tape. The net result is that the excess glue residue is now at most 1/8" wide, and it can be removed with a card scraper before it fully hardens. It's important to wash and then completely dry the card scraper after doing this, because a glue film will interfere with its efficiency, and rust will pit it.

To preserve an iron's edge, remove most of the hardened glue before reaching for the plane. An old-fashioned paint scraper, sharpened quickly on a belt sander or grindstone, is a great way to remove glue squeeze out.

Get comfortable. Spread your feet. Stance is important because it determines how much control you have over the tool being used. If you have to reach too far across a board to complete a pass, the plane will tip at the end of its journey. By lowering the work, you lengthen your arms. Work that is secured to the top of a workbench that is too tall is awkward to reach properly, and therefore it is difficult to control the plane.

Make passes in a rhythmic mode. That is, the plane should already be up to speed by the time the cutter meets the surface. The stroke begins with the front (toe) of the plane on the work, when the throat still hasn't arrived. Downward pressure is applied at the knob, and the tote (handle) is used to steer. Pushing down too hard on the tote causes the plane to drag, robbing the stroke of its momentum. Allow the tool to do its work. All those millions of carpenters who preceded shop machinery and relied only on hand planes would never have made it through a long workday if all their energy was used up pushing a plane. It doesn't take force to work a bench plane. It takes good tuning and good control.

Begin the actual flattening process with a scrub plane, but only if necessary. Retard the iron to begin with, and slowly extend it if the results are less than expected. It's a good idea to check each change in the set by taking a couple of passes on a scrap board of the same species. If the iron extends too far, the plane will dig into the work, or chatter. The stroke must be continuous

Scrub planes are fairly violent, especially when used across the grain. They can leave gouges that are difficult to remove. Planing at about 15° off grain direction works best.

and fluid. Don't allow the plane to stutter. At the beginning of the stroke, the toe alone should touch the work. As the plane advances, the heel is lowered to the work so that the aggressive iron is already in motion when it meets the wood. At the end of the stroke, lift the heel gradually to extricate the iron and feather the cut. It takes a little practice, and the movements are slight and easy rather than dramatic. Work primarily with the grain, but don't be afraid to go diagonally. Cutting across the grain will result in tear-out, and the resultant gouging is more difficult to clean up later on.

After the scrub plane has removed most of the really high spots, switch to a long plane. This can be a fore or a jackplane, although on very wide boards a jointer is the best choice.

Again, get comfortable and spread your feet for a solid stance. These should be short strokes, but be sure they can be completed without feeling that your body is tipping. Begin with more pressure on the toe, and end with more pressure on the heel of the plane.

As with the scrub plane, begin with the lightest cut possible. Give the plane a few passes to pare the high spots—these have to be removed before you begin to see shavings. Work at a diagonal, first moving to your left, and then to your right. Skew the plane as well as the stroke. That is, hold the plane at about 15° or 20° to the stroke direction, and move the plane across the board at about the same angle to the grain. The result here is that the cutting edge of the iron meets the grain at about 45°. At times, it may be necessary to skew even further than this, but the grain will soon begin to complain about your work habits, tearing rather than slicing the wood. Increase the depth of cut slightly if shavings begin to disappear.

After the scrub, switch to a longer plane and begin with a light cut. A jack (No. 5) is ideal. Hold the plane at 15° or 20° to the stroke while moving across the board at about the same angle to the grain.

Stop every few strokes to check your progress with the straightedge and winding sticks. The idea here is to go no further than necessary and avoid creating new low spots. With the straightedge, check a number of different diagonals, looking for light between the steel and the wood. Mark high spots with a pencil, and address these with the plane. Check for twists with

The jack renders the board flat. The smoother then cleans up after the jack. Set the iron to take very thin cuts and work along the grain, holding the plane at about a 15° skew.

the winding sticks, laying them across the board a little bit in from each end, and then standing back a few feet and sight across them to see how they line up. This is a relative measurement, rather than a finite one. It can't really be quantified (called out in terms of inches), and this is an important concept. Choose the stick that is closest to the desired level, and then mark the board where the other stick indicates that more flattening is needed.

When the board is flat, switch to a smoothing plane to clean up the marks made by the larger plane. Make sure the corners of the iron (if not its entire width) are crowned. (A smoothing plane's iron should always be slightly crowned, especially at the outside edges, to avoid leaving any telltale trails on the wood, as discussed in Chapter 6.) Again, set the iron to take the smallest cut possible. This time, work along the grain rather than across it. In other words, the stroke should follow the grain, but the plane itself can still be skewed a little. The advantage here is that a slight skew allows the cutting edge to slice across the grain as the plane

History of Hand Planes
William Marples & Sons

This company is still a familiar name for woodworkers who buy chisels and other hand tools. It was founded by William Marples in Sheffield, England in 1829, and several similar works were successively started by other family members, including his brothers and heirs. The original company traded under a brand called Shamrock, which was an unusual logo for an English firm, given the state of Anglo-Irish politics at the time (British-ruled Ireland was enduring a series of famines that eventually led to mass migration to America in the 1840s). Marples produced limited numbers of hand planes.

In 1962, the original William Marples & Sons became part of the Record Tool Company. A second line, founded by Joseph Marples, is still family owned. (At one point, there were actually seven Marples companies producing hand tools in Sheffield, and not all of them got along.) The Joseph Marples branch moved into a new factory in 2001.

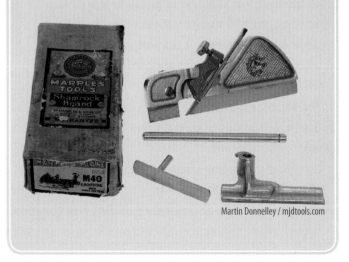

Martin Donnelley / mjdtools.com

moves forward. Keep in mind that the function here is to clean up or smooth the surface, rather than flatten it. The fewer strokes needed, the better.

When the board looks and feels flat and smooth, and the straightedge and winding sticks agree with your assessment, it's time to check your work with a raking light. This means nothing more than aligning one edge or end of the board with a light source (a shop work light, or even daylight through a window).

When the source of the light is on the same plane as the surface of the wood, or slightly above it, any imperfections cast minute shadows and become much easier to see. Mark these with a pencil and then address them with a card scraper (see Chapter 4).

In most cases, a board being flattened with a hand plane is too wide for the jointer. However, most will not be too wide for even the smallest (12½" wide) benchtop thickness planer. With one face now flat, the second face can be made flat with a couple of passes through the planer. If it's wider than the planer bed, repeat the process outlined above to flatten the second face, or find a shop with a wider planer or even a wide belt sander. (Check for cabinet shops in the phone book. Most of them will run boards through machines for their standard shop rate, with a minimum charge for 15 minutes.) Also, keep in mind the old adage, "Keep it as long as you can for as long as you can." Don't trim the boards or panels to length until after they have been machined, as many planers (not all, but many) leave snipe in their wake. Snipe means that the first and last three inches or so of the board comes out a little thinner than the rest of the board. It's caused when the board is only being held down by one roller (the one on the infeed side) at the beginning of the cut, so it tips up a little and the knives take more than their fair share. As the board moves forward and contacts the outfeed roller too, it is pushed down flat on the table and the snipe disappears. This process happens in reverse at the end of the board's travel through the planer. When it leaves the infeed roller, it bounces up into the blade. So, allow for snipe.

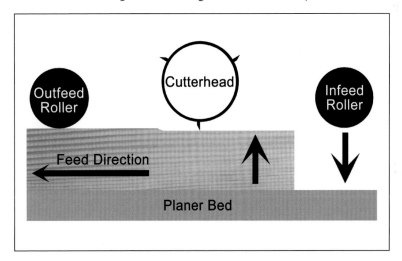

If boards will be passed through an electric planer, allow a few extra inches in their length for snipe, a depression a few inches long that is created when the board passes the downward pressure of the infeed roller.

If the board is a panel for a door, and it will be machined down to something like ½" or ¼" thickness, it will probably be more aesthetically pleasing to use the hand planed face as the front of the panel, leaving the machined face at the back. Of course, the choice will be influenced by the color and grain of the wood, but a hand planed panel is definitely worth framing.

Chapter 9
How to Joint the Edge of a Board

Why use a hand plane to joint?

Jointing is the process of squaring up two edges so that they can be glued together in a butt joint with no gaps. When preparing for edge-gluing, an electric jointer does a pretty good job of flattening the edges of two boards. Or does it? There are three big problems with electric jointers that make a hand plane look like a great option.

First off, the infeed table on a jointer is adjusted up and down to change the depth of cut, and all that movement eventually has some effect on the machine. In the average home shop, very few jointers actually have both tables on exactly the same plane. That is, if one places a long steel straightedge on the tables, they usually don't line up exactly parallel along their entire lengths. The infeed table, the one in front of the knives, either pitches (falls a little as it approaches the knives), or heaves (rises as it gets closer to the knives). If two boards are jointed on most electric jointers and then the jointed edges are butted up against each other, the degree of error is immediately obvious. If there is a gap at each of the ends, the infeed table is pitched. A gap in the middle of the boards means that the infeed table is heaving. Fortunately, this is an easy fix as there are usually a couple of adjustment bolts at one end, underneath the infeed table. But just fixing a pitch or heave doesn't make the case for this machine.

This wooden jointer, made by Peck & Crouch in New England around 1850, is enjoying a useful second life after having been fitted with a new Hock iron and chipbreaker.

The second problem with jointers is mill marking. A board that is run across an electric jointer meets the knives so many times that it seems the cut is constant. However, the jointer actually leaves a series of cut marks on the board. Most small-shop, three-knife jointers make roughly 10,000 cuts per minute. That's about 167 cuts per second. If a board is passed across

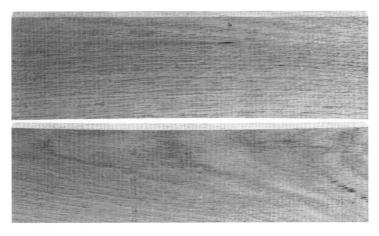

If two boards jointed on an electric jointer have a gap at the ends, the infeed table is tilting as it approached the knives. A gap in the middle of the boards (shown) means that the infeed table is rising near the knives.

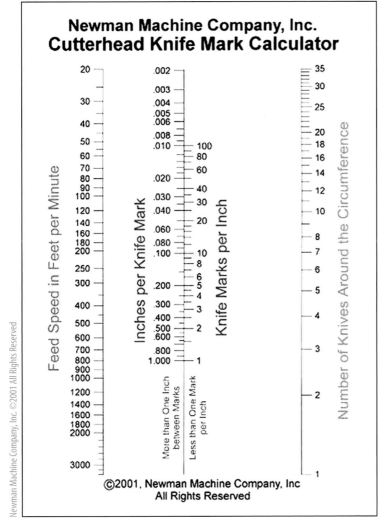

To calculate the number of mill marks per inch on a board, place one end of a straightedge on the Number of Knives in your cutterhead and the other on the Feed Speed, and read the Knife Marks per Inch.

that jointer at a feed rate of one foot every two seconds (30 feet per minute, which is about normal), the surface of the board is only being cut twenty-eight times every inch. That cutting interval of $\frac{1}{28}$" is actually not very fine. Newman Machine Company, Inc. of Greensboro, North Carolina, provides the industry with a host of large milling machinery. Their guidelines are 7–8 marks per inch for rough planing in hardwoods, and 15 to 25 marks for finish planing. In our example, there are 28 small ridges across every inch of the board along its entire length. Feeding the stock more slowly will increase the number of cuts, but most of us in the real world work as fast as the example above. So, we need to use hand planes to clean up the milling marks.

The third problem with mechanical jointers is that many of them have short fences that are not absolutely rigid. The lack of height means that wide boards can tip a little, and they end up being a degree or more out of square. Even though the edge of a board is usually quite narrow (in the vicinity of ¾"), it must be completely square to the face of the board along its entire length. For good joinery, it shouldn't deviate along either its length or its width. If it tips a bit, there's not much point in making the edge straight along its entire length: When it is married to another board to create a wider panel at glue-up, there's a

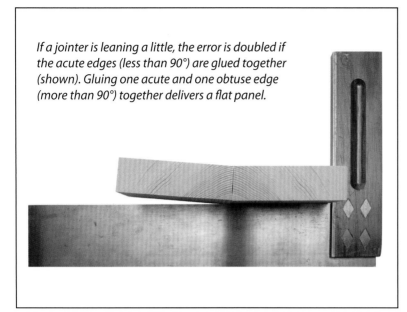

If a jointer is leaning a little, the error is doubled if the acute edges (less than 90°) are glued together (shown). Gluing one acute and one obtuse edge (more than 90°) together delivers a flat panel.

gap at the top or bottom of the joint because one or both edges weren't square. In other words, the two edges don't add up to 180°. If an adjustable jointer fence is leaning at an angle of even 1°, the boards will form a 178° angle on one face, and a 182° angle on the other. One can flip one of the boards over to correct the problem, but wouldn't it be nice to get it right?

A jointer, fore or jackplane can do the job.

Choose a Jointer

The jointer planes (No. 7 and No. 8) and the fore plane (No. 6) are all used to dress edges. These are sometimes called try planes. It's a loose term, most often applied to the No. 6. All three can also be used to flatten the face of a board, but they are especially renowned and valued for edge work. They range from 18" to 24" long. When a board that's less than two feet long is being worked, a jackplane is adequate for jointing its edge— a No. 8 would be unwieldy. So, the first thing to consider is length. The longer the board, the longer the plane should be. The one exception here is that woodworkers who are of small stature may have a hard time using very large planes. If a plane is too big to handle comfortably, it will be difficult to control. Using

geometry to gain a mechanical advantage sometimes helps. Try lowering the work below bench height so that the edge being worked is at about waist level. Clamping one end in a bench vise and supporting the other with a sawhorse often works. Independent supports such as Black & Decker's Workmate® will also secure the work at a comfortable height.

Next, consider the cutting angle. This is the angle at which the iron is bedded combined with the angle that has been ground on the bevel. In the trade, this is known as an included angle, a term that woodworkers borrowed from geometry teachers who tell us that when two lines meet at a common point called the vertex, the angle between them is known as the included angle.

A low angle works better in dense stock, and a high angle with a shallow cut is more suited to wild grain. Because of this, many fine woodworkers own a few different jointers and keep them set up with different cutting angles. Stanley's traditional jointer planes have a bedding angle of 45°. That is, the iron is held at 45° to the surface being planed. On the edges of boards, this time-tested formula works well for

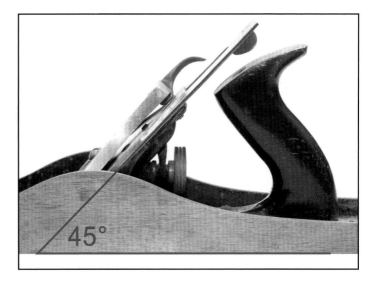

Most jointer planes have their iron bedded at 45°, with the bevel down. If the bevel was up and the iron was sharpened at 25°, the combined cutting angle would be 70°, an angle which would scrape rather than plane wood.

most woods. But it isn't always an ideal bed, especially in dense, heavy hardwoods and, most noticeably, in those with meandering grain where tear-out is an issue. When tear-out has to be fixed on boards that are already close to their final dimensions, we sometimes have to discard the board or else re-size the entire project—so it's something to be avoided.

There are planes available with pitches that differ from the Stanley. Veritas Tools, Inc. makes a superb bevel-up jointer which has the ability to change the included angle by changing the irons. That is, the iron can be swapped for one with a different bevel angle. In normal work, the plane's 12° bedding angle is coupled with a standard 25° blade bevel for an effective cutting angle of 37°, which minimizes tearing in most woods. But the company also offers optional 38° and 50° bevel blades for this plane. According to Veritas, "the 38° bevel blade yields an effective cutting angle of 50° (commonly known as a York pitch) and is excellent for general smoothing. The 50° bevel blade is best for working difficult or reversing grain, and the combined cutting angle of 62° (that is, 50° bevel plus 12° bedding) produces a Type II chip that eliminates tear-out." A 38° toothed blade is also available for working difficult grain, especially knots.

The low-angle Veritas jointer uses a very thick bevel-up iron and a 12° bed angle. When an iron with a 25° bevel is used, the combined cutting angle is 37°, which is 9° less than a Stanley.

Knight Toolworks offers wooden planes in Ipe, padouk, or purpleheart with irons that can be ordered with a bedding angle of 45°, 47°, 50°, 55°, or 60°. Their jack and jointer planes are set at 47° unless a customer requests a different angle, and their entire bench plane line has sliding adjustable mouths.

In jointing, the only requirement for the width of the iron is that it must be wider than the edge of the board. Sometimes, planing at a slight skew helps handle hard grain. The net effect of skewing the plane while jointing is that it slightly increases the pitch while decreasing the width of the cutting edge. It also allows for a slicing action that reduces friction.

Another exciting option is offered by Lie-Nielsen Toolworks, which is their High Angle Frog (HAF). According to the company, "all Stanley-type bench plane irons are bedded at 45°, or common pitch. But the famous English smoothers like Norris are usually 50° (York Pitch) or 55° (Middle Pitch). The higher pitches make smoothing difficult wood easier. Our unique High Angle Frogs quickly convert our No. 4 and No. 4½ Smoother to York or Middle Pitch. These frogs will also fit our other planes with 2" or 2⅜" blades." That includes their jointers. Unfortunately, the HAF frogs won't fit other makes of planes. The High Angle Frogs may be ordered as an extra option, or installed in a plane you already own.

The Jointing Sequence

It's good practice to first flatten the wide faces of a board and then work on making the edges straight and true. The reasoning here is that one can lay a square on one of

History of Hand Planes
Alexander Mathieson & Son

Two members of this family made infill planes in Dundee, Scotland, in the nineteenth century. The father, Alexander Mathieson, was a master craftsman and a poor businessman who founded the company sometime around 1820. His son, Thomas, grew the company dramatically from the 1850s on. He managed to take over several competitors, including the biggest firm in Edinburgh (J&W Stewart). Eventually, Mathieson & Son became the biggest manufacturer of hand planes in British history. Later on, under the guidance of John Manners, the company made some magnificent molding planes with multiple irons.

Infill plane production continued well into the 1950s, although the planes began to take second place to a line of large auger bits used in railway construction. In 1957, the company was purchased by Sheffield-based Ridgeway Tools, Ltd., and it was subsequently absorbed into Record-Ridgeway, where it quietly faded away.

Larry Meeker / Patented-Antiques.com

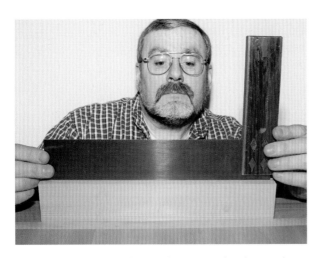

Several times during planing, lay a straightedge on the board and check for gaps that indicate where an extra pass or two may be required. Retard the iron for a smaller cut as the board approaches flat.

the flat faces to check that the edges are at 90° to that established plane. So, once a board is flat, the edges can be worked.

When jointing the first edge, the board should be quite a bit wider (not thicker) than the desired final dimension. There should be at least ¼" of waste available, and hopefully more.

For woodworkers who have never used a jointer, it's critical to practice jointing on a scrap board before working on a part for an actual project. These big, heavy planes can tip easily, and sometimes they even lean a little without our noticing. It takes a little practice to get the feel of them.

Secure the board on edge in a bench vise equipped with wooden jaws. Alternately, clamp the board in a metal vise with thin stock on either side of the board to protect the previously worked wide faces. Place a straightedge along the edge to be planed and look at the line where the board and the straightedge meet. Using this method you can quickly locate the high and low spots. Placing a background light behind the board also helps. Use a pencil to mark the high spots. Hold the pencil at an angle and use the wide edge of the lead, rather than the thin point, so it doesn't dig in. The marks that you make will disappear as the board is trued, indicating how much more work has to be done after each pass.

Assuming that the plane doesn't need to be tuned or sharpened, set it for a very thin depth of cut and take a couple of passes along the edge of the board. Then use a square to check the edge across its width. This gives you a good indication of whether the plane is being held at 90° to the face. Check every few inches along the edge, because the cut will change as your stance changes. Holding the plane at 90° is actually a lot easier than one might think. Woodworkers quickly develop an instinct for this when they start checking the edge with a square. If in doubt, fences are available (see page 73).

When a plane is held slightly tilted in one direction on a first pass, and then held slightly tipped in the other direction (a matter of over-compensation) on the next pass, the edge becomes crowned. This phenomenon is called

People aren't machines and we tend to lean in one direction or the other. When jointing, check the edge of a board several times to make sure that the plane is being held at 90° during each pass.

"camber"—in engineering the term is often used to describe how a road is slightly crowned so that water runs off equally on either side. As woodworkers rarely have to deal with run-off, camber on an edge isn't a desirable facet. The way to avert it is to achieve consistency: Hold the plane the same way every time, and use the same body position, or stance, over and over again (just like golf).

Stance and Stroke

Stance is more important with a jointer than with any other plane. That's because it takes a great deal of energy and strength to glide these heavy planes smoothly along an edge without tipping side-to-side. Also, a jointer is usually the only plane that requires a woodworker to move his or her feet during the stroke. The sheer weight of the plane

When learning how to use a jointer plane, it's easy to lean in one direction on a pass and then overcompensate in the other direction on the next. The result is that the edge of the board becomes rounded, or cambered.

can be an issue at the beginning and end of each cut too, when the cast iron body is cantilevered off the end of the board and unsupported for a second or two. If the work is held too high on the bench, all bets are off: we simply can't control such a large tool at arm's length, or standing on our toes. If possible, your dominant eye should be directly above the board, looking down on the plane so you can determine if it is leaning in one direction or the other. To determine your

Our brain chooses one of our eyes to be dominant, a fact well known to people who shoot rifles. If this eye is directly above the plane while jointing it helps eliminate the tendency to lean left or right.

At the beginning of the stroke, the body should be positioned so that the tote is in line with the trailing shoulder. As the arm loses power and control, the tote moves forward to compensate.

dominant eye, pretend that you are shooting a rifle and see which eye you like to keep open when looking through your imaginary scope.

At the beginning of the stroke, your body should be positioned so that the shoulders create an angle of 30° or so with the line of the work (the top of the board). This angle will open slightly as the stroke develops. The handle (tote) should be in line with your trailing shoulder. On a right-handed person,who works from right to left, this will be the right shoulder. The

tote shouldn't be behind the body, as the arm holding it loses more and more power and control the further back it goes. As the stroke develops, the tote moves forward a little in its relationship to the your body. Don't reach too far ahead as this, too, reduces control.

Unlike that of shorter planes, the stroke with a jointer is often several feet long. That means that you need to take a walk alongside the board to complete it. Your path should be clear, with no hoses, cords or debris on the floor, and it should be uninterrupted by benches, machines or other obstacles. Reaching around something in the path will definitely create camber (that's the hump in the highway), or a tilt in one direction.

Veritas has developed a jointer fence for their Bailey-style bench planes that keeps the sole at 90°. This fence can be adapted to fit other planes with a little ingenuity.

Jointer Fences

The biggest problem that new woodworkers have when jointing an edge is keeping the plane's sole at 90° to the wide face of the board. Veritas Tools Inc. has developed a wonderful accessory for their long bench planes that addresses this, and they call it what it is: a Jointer Fence. It doesn't work on the Veritas bevel-up jointer and smoother planes (there's a special version for them), but it fits their standard long planes. With a little work, this simple device can be adapted to work with larger planes from most other manufacturers.

The Veritas Jointer Fence is made of anodized aluminum and measures 11" long and 2" tall. Its function is to help a

There's a special version of the jointer fence that can be quickly attached to the Veritas bevel-up jointer and smoother planes. All it takes is tightening a couple of knurled brass knobs.

The Veritas fences are offset so that they take into account the small distance between the side of the cutter and the edge of the plane body.

woodworker plane edges that are perfectly square to the face of the work. (For advanced woodworkers, it can also be used to shoot angles that are less than 90° by using a beveled wooden guide.) Rare-earth magnets make the jointer fence quick and easy to attach or remove, and it can be used on either side of all sizes of their bench planes—from a No. 4 smooth plane to a No. 8 jointer.

The fence attaches to a plane using magnets that are embedded in the aluminum fence. A small set screw is then tightened into a hole in the wing (side) of the plane, and this stops it sliding back and forth. This hole will need to be located, drilled and threaded in planes not made by Veritas. If the fence isn't exactly at 90° to the sole (sometimes wings are a little off), the lateral adjustment on the iron is used to correct this. For a perfect cut, the cutting edge of the iron needs to be at 90° to the fence. That is, the relationship between the fence and the iron is more important than that between the fence and the sole.

Jointing Two Boards

Sometimes when boards are jointed, it doesn't really matter if they are a degree or so off a perfect 90. The edge of a shelf, for example, needs to look like it's perfect but it doesn't need to be perfect. At other times, though, we are jointing boards so that they can be edge-glued to create a wider board or a large part. So, here's an old shop trick. If we clamp two boards together in the vise and joint both at the same time, there's a real advantage to this. If the plane is accidentally held a degree or two off, the boards can be opened like a book and the two jointed surfaces will then describe a perfect 180° angle. One edge will be a degree or so over 90, and the other will be a degree or so under 90. The errors will offset each other. The math is simple: 89+91=180.

By clamping two boards in the vise and jointing them at the same time, it doesn't matter if the plane is at exactly 90° or not. The boards can be opened as if there was a hinge at the jointed edges, to form a perfect 180°.

Chapter 10

How to Work with Difficult Grain

I can hear them already. An angry mob of purists, torches burning, chants resounding as they march up the long, dark hill to my workshop. Lightning crackles overhead as the wind washes their ugly expletives. Hopefully, nobody remembered to bring a rope. For what I am about to say, they will never forgive me...

Sometimes, sanding is the answer.

Anybody who has ever built furniture knows the comfort of straight, predictable quartersawn grain when it comes to stiles, rails and legs. But in tops, doors and side panels, figured wood can add a degree of drama that simply takes one's breath away. Unfortunately, that lively grain often wanders in every direction and can be quite difficult to control. When planed, it can chip, tear and peel, presenting the cutting edge with a mix of end, reversing or side grains—sometimes all three in the same stroke.

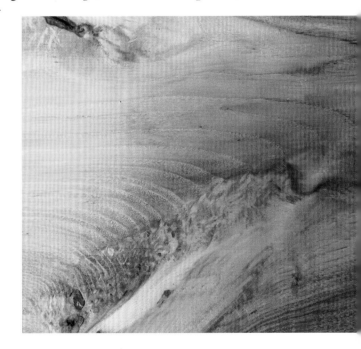

Flattening a panel in grain that has so much personality is always a compromise. Often, the best we can hope for is to plane about ⅔ of the way, and finish up with a sander.

However, there is hope. The right mix of planes and blade settings can often complete the job and deliver an iridescent, lustrous, even shimmering surface that leaps to life when the right light strikes it. Sometimes, unfortunately, we need to compromise, and run the panel through a drum or wide belt sander. Sanding takes the edge off the finish because it fills the open cells with dust and crushes the cell sidewalls, rather than slicing across them as a plane will do.

So, when do we stop planing and start sanding? Wood with difficult grain is often expensive, sometimes irreplaceable and almost always holds a personal value, so common sense tells us not to destroy or waste it. If there's a spare piece to practice on, then by all means haul out the planes and go to work. If there isn't, then each occasion demands a separate decision. There really are no rules of thumb. If you are confident enough in your own craft, or want to learn a new skill, let's start planing.

Get the Planes Ready

It's usually not a good idea to run this kind of lively grain through a thickness planer, as the grain often changes direction and the knives of a planer will chip it, creating deep pockets that simply can't be fixed. That leaves hand planes or a wide belt sander as the two remaining thickness options. Chapter 8 discusses the former.

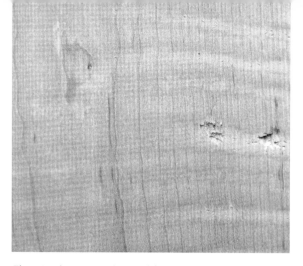

Electric planers work wood from a single direction, often leaving large pockets and divots in figured wood that has grain running in several directions. A hand plane doesn't have this limitation.

When working with wild grain, the condition of each tool is critical. See Chapters 6 and 7 for guidance on tuning the plane and sharpening the iron. The sole must be flat, the iron must be razor sharp and the chipbreaker should be set about 1/16" shy of the cutting edge. Honing a small secondary bevel at about 28° on a 25° ground bevel is also a good idea.

To help plane tricky grain (and here we're talking about the wide faces of boards and not just the narrow edges), heavy plane bodies really help. A cast iron plane seems to work better than a wooden body (although the user's skill and experience make a lot of difference). Heavy irons such as Ron Hock's blades or those made by Lie-Nielsen Toolworks definitely make a difference, as does a tight mouth. That is, the throat should be closed to the smallest opening that will permit waste to pass through. A well-tuned chipbreaker, properly set, is essential, and a heavier one (available from Hock Tools) will virtually eliminate chatter.

If a great deal of material must be removed, begin with a scrub plane. Start with a small cut. If this aggressive tool has a tendency to tear the grain, try retarding the iron even further to see if the results improve. The stroke must be continuous (no stopping and starting). Try changing direction, too. Slicing diagonally across the board produces different results than running straight along it. If the plane is still digging holes and creating more problems than it solves, it may be time to do the unthinkable. Reach for a belt sander with a coarse abrasive (60 grit, or even 36 grit if there's a lot of stock to remove). This is a reversal of the normal, logical sequence, where we begin with planes and, if there are problems, switch to sandpaper. Here, use the coarse belt to cut away most of the waste and then return to planes to finesse the surface.

A cast iron plane seems to produce less chatter on wild grain than a wooden bodied plane. A heavy iron and chip-breaker also make a difference, as does a small mouth opening.

On particularly wild grain, it may be okay to do the unthinkable. A belt sander with a coarse abrasive will cut away most of the waste. Planes and cabinet scrapers can then finesse the surface.

With most of the waste removed, a No. 5 jackplane is the next in line. Skew the plane so the cutting edge slices across the grain, rather than straight into it. Skewing actually adds a few degrees to the bed. A few manufacturers make a high angle jack, and Lie-Nielsen Toolworks offers an optional High Angle Frog that converts the blade angle from 45° to 50°, or York pitch. The elevated iron makes smoothing in difficult woods easier. Other custom builders offer either wooden or infill planes that are comparable in size to a jack, and come with a York or higher bedding. But a standard 45° Stanley, especially one equipped with a heavy aftermarket iron that has been properly sharpened, will handle all but the most undisciplined grain pattern.

The jack's main job is to remove evidence of the scrub plane, and then to begin the leveling process. With the jack's restricted length (14") and the width of its iron (2"), it won't be able to complete the job. For that, we switch to a jointer. The sheer size of this largest of planes ensures that it rides across the high spots and erases them, leveling the surface in short order. Again, we're only after flatness here, and not a finished surface. The jointer may have to be skewed to handle some grain patterns, but the momentum provided by its weight and mass is a mechanical advantage.

When cleaning up after a scrub plane on figured wood, the jack needs to choose a path that follows the changing grain direction. Steering through the grain helps avoid chipping, especially in endgrain.

When working difficult grain, the jack is often followed by a jointer set for a very light cut. This long plane levels out the high spots and doesn't dig into wild grain as easily as a smaller plane.

By upgrading inexpensive smoothing planes (like the Stanley shown here) with a decent aftermarket iron and chip breaker, they work surprisingly well on wild grain.

Stanley Tools

Stanley's new, heavy, No. 4 smoother will be released in late 2009 or early 2010, and it carries the old Sweetheart logo from the 1920s. With a heavy iron and chipbreaker, it may well begin a new era in planes.

The Smoother

With the board essentially flat, switch to a smoother. This can be a relatively inexpensive plane. Stanley, Anant, Groz and others offer models under $50, and several companies including Grizzly (item H0635) and Sears Craftsman (item 00937178000) have smoothers that cost even less than that. By upgrading these inexpensive planes with a good tune-up and a decent aftermarket iron and chipbreaker, they work surprisingly well on wild grain. However, they will never feel quite as good as a high-quality plane such as a Lie-Nielsen, Veritas, or a British Clifton, and they won't perform as well. By the way, a company called Preston, which was later acquired by Record Tools in 1932, originally made Clifton planes. The design copyrights were later sold to Clico Tooling, who now manufactures them as Clifton planes in Sheffield, England. They are based on the classic Stanley Bedrock planes from before World War II.

Record still sells a line of planes under their own name in the UK, but they are less expensive and, in my opinion, of much lower quality than the Cliftons. Speaking of quality, Stanley's new No. 4 smoother (not yet released at presstime) promises to be a very useful and refined plane. It's part of a premium line of tools (two block planes, the smoother, a shoulder plane and a low-angle jack) that borrow the old Sweetheart logo from the 1920s, and the company believes they will compete favorably with Veritas, Lie-Nielsen and other top-notch manufacturers.

Handling difficult grain is all about control. Hold the smoother lightly, and listen to it. Pushing down too hard or making fast and furious strokes will only hide what's happening. The plane will accelerate or decelerate according to the grain patterns, and this is how it tells us what to do. Begin by setting a crowned or radiused iron (see Chapter 6) so that it is absolutely even across its width. If one side is projecting past the sole more than the other, the plane will leave heartbreaking trails across the surface. The cut should be very minimal. Here, in difficult

History of Hand Planes
Millers Falls (1861-1982)

Charles Amidon and Levi Gunn, who both worked for the Greenfield Tool Company, founded this enterprise during the Civil War. They began making hand-cranked rollers for washing machines, and added braces, miter boxes, hand drills and saws over the next few years. Surprisingly, their first planes were not added until 1929, when the company astounded the market by introducing almost four dozen models all at once, half of them bench planes. They were very similar to Stanley models, and they were both well made and well finished. Although they might be judged as a mite gaudy today, at the time their nickel-plated lever caps, red frogs and rosewood totes were received with enthusiasm, and the planes sold well for a long time. One difference between these and Stanley models was a jointed lever cap, invented by employee Charlie Fox, that contacted the chipbreaker/iron subassembly at three points, rather than two.

Ten years after introducing the plane line, Millers Falls equipped their No. 209 smoother with a red plastic handle and tote, and upgraded the body from nickel to chrome. The futuristic look delivered by this combination lasted until 1948, when the 209 was retired and the company introduced the 709 with a more solid-looking red plastic handle made of tenite, and a sleeker, more space-age look. This became the company's famous Buck Rogers look. In 1962, Millers Falls was absorbed by the Ingersoll-Rand Company.

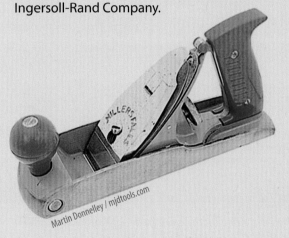

Martin Donnelley / mjdtools.com

grain, we're looking for a translucent, evenly cut, very thin shaving that is the full width of the exposed iron.

Perhaps the biggest mistake among new hand tool users is impatience: they tend to set the iron so aggressively that even the most in-tune and well-sharpened plane has no choice but to chatter. When it comes to having a pleasant experience with bench planes, this point can't be overstressed. If you sight down the sole from the front and can clearly see the iron, it is probably extended too far. In the image of two curled shavings shown on page 80, the thick one on top shows evidence that the chipbreaker needed to continually break the shaving to make it curl out of the mouth of the plane. The lower (and thinner) shaving shows much less stress, and it left a

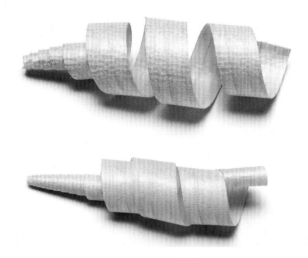

When most of a board is on the bench but some is off the edge and unsupported, there's a chance the work will tip or move, causing damage as it is planed. If possible, support the entire board.

far smoother surface. The lesson here is that, in most cases, we need to take the thinnest shaving possible.

I run my fingers from the heel (back) to the toe (front) of the sole—first down one side of the sole and then down the other—to feel how much cutter is exposed. (Running the other way would slice the fingers!) Once a woodworker gets a feel for this, he or she can quickly decide how much to extend or retard the iron for a perfect cut. Less exposed blade means less work to move the plane and less tear-out in tough grain, and these add up to more success and more pleasure. Less truly is more. If necessary, advance the iron a little, but never a lot.

Spread your feet for a solid, reliable stance. A feeling of imbalance or insecurity means that your mind is dealing with equilibrium, and is not free to listen to the plane. Its okay to cantilever the work off the edge of the bench, but the unsupported part should be no more than about 15% of the board's overall width. Cantilevering allows the woodworker to stand closer to the work and lean in over it. Working at arm's length, we lose control. Working behind our shoulder, we lose control. The ideal stroke is between our shoulders. People with bad backs may want to try securing the board so that it tips a little toward them. This reduces the reach, and therefore the amount one bends—reducing both strain and stretching. Those with chronic pain might consider using Japanese planes, which are pulled rather than pushed. It's a completely different set of motions and it uses muscles in reverse. Traditionally, Japanese artisans worked on the floor and kneeled on the board, or secured the wood in very low benches so they could sit over it. Americans report a far higher incidence of back pain than the Japanese, which of course has nothing whatsoever to do with planing, but it's an interesting comment on the two lifestyles. For detailed information on traditional Japanese woodworking and tools, see Toshio Odate's book, *Japanese Woodworking Tools* (Linden Publishing, 1998).

A Strong Stroke

The stroke is the next consideration. Planing shouldn't be comparable to John Henry racing a steam engine. It is a measured, controlled exercise that combines a rhythmic repetition with constant interpretation. Each stroke is separate, beginning and ending as a complete unit. Yet, each stroke is also part of a pattern: as the muscles of the hands and back and arms are synchronized, the body becomes accustomed to the sequence and wishes to maintain it. By listening to the plane, we know how far to move it after one stroke in preparation for the next: The previous stroke tells us whether the plane was tilted, or the end grain along the left side of the cut presented more resistance than the long grain on the right side, and so on.

It is virtually impossible to do a good job of planing in the absence of a raking light, and in wild grain that light becomes even more valuable because it points out errant fibers, highlighting them by casting long shadows that exaggerate their size.

Pick a direction. Or several. To avoid tear-out, the stroke should follow the grain as much as possible, and in a crotch or other wild grain, that may be more than one direction. Look at the side of the board. At the beginning of the stroke, the grain along the side should be lower than it is at the end of the stroke. It should rise along the length of the stroke and meet the cutter at the end.

Use the knob and tote to your best advantage. At the beginning of the stroke, apply more downward pressure (but still not a lot) on the knob. By the end of the stroke, that downward pressure should now be greater at the tote. The tote is the rudder, and it controls skew and direction. Too much downward pressure will interfere with its ability to steer.

A raking light (one placed close to the surface so that the light washes across the work) will create shadows that quickly pinpoint trouble spots such as dents, hollows, high points and mill marks.

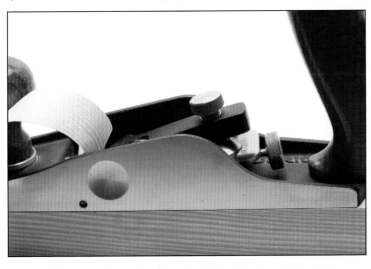

To avoid tear-out, the grain along the side of the board should be lower at the beginning of the stroke than it is at the end. Otherwise the cut may follow the grain. Sometimes, a board must be worked from both ends.

History of Hand Planes
T. Norris & Son

Although it was not the largest producer of infill planes in Britain, T. Norris & Son earned a reputation as one of the finest plane makers in history. From 1860 until World War II, the company made a line of superior tools that were coveted by fine craftsmen. Norris planes on average cost between three and four times the price of a comparable Stanley. While they initially produced smoothing, bull-nose, shoulder, rabbet and other planes, the line settled to smoothers and a few others by the advent of World War II. The bodies were either cast iron or dovetailed steel, with walnut, ebony and rosewood infills. Most coveted were the steel models, where the sides and sole were joined with a double dovetail joint that can't physically be made in wood: The tails were cut long and then hammered back to fit, and then they were ground and filed for a perfect fit. The same method was used by

Konrad Sauer / sauerandsteiner.com

three other major infill plane manufacturers, Preston, Spiers and Mathieson.

What separated Norris from the pack was their clever lateral and vertical blade adjuster. Patented in 1913, this used a single lever to make both adjustments to the plane's iron. Before this, infill planes were adjusted by tapping them with a hammer (as most of the competition were forced to continue to do, because of the patent). Norris thrived while the others began to fade, but the success was relatively short-lived. By the outbreak of war, the company was down to a handful of employees, and demand for much less expensive mass-produced planes had eroded its market share.

If you don't end the stroke before the plane reaches the far side of the board it will tear out the edge.

Rotate the board to work the missed area near that far edge.

On knots, there are a couple of ways to go. Sometimes the wood within the knot isn't very hard, and it will plane satisfactorily with a smoother. Sometimes one has to switch to a sharp, low angle block plane to work the core, and then revert to the smoother or a card scraper to even up the surrounding wood. Attack it from several angles with the block plane, and, if it won't surrender, try slicing across the knot at a very acute angle. A low-angle block plane also works well in places where the grain changes direction too quickly for the larger smoothing plane to handle.

Here, use short, small strokes to pare rather than cut the surface.

After the smoother does its work, wild grain can be tamed with either a scraping plane or a card scraper. A sharp scraper is a wonder to behold on end grain and wild grain, as it eliminates any evidence that the smoother was used. See Chapter 4 for information on tuning and using a scraper. After scraping, use the raking light to check for scratches. If necessary, sand with 280, 320 and 400 grit papers, in that order. If the 280 grit paper isn't removing visible scratches, go back to the card scraper for a while.

Knots cause endgrain that protrudes through side grain, so they are usually harder than the surrounding wood. But they can often be tackled with a low-angle block plane and a card scraper.

A sharp card scraper or a scraping plane works well on end grain and wild grain. Its burr shears small fibers and eliminates any evidence that the smoother was used.

Chapter 11

How to Mill Rabbets

Stanley's No. 78

With the efficiency of table saw dado heads and plunge router bits, it's a rare thing to find anyone using a hand plane to cut rabbets or dadoes anymore. That's unfortunate, as there are few shop activities as rewarding as planing a rabbet with an old No. 78. It takes just a few seconds to set the fence and depth control, and most rabbets can be cut in less time than setting up a router table and making the cut with a machine. No noise, no dust, just beautiful thin shavings floating to the floor.

A rabbet is essentially just a shelf along one edge or end of a board—a groove that's missing one of its sidewalls. A rabbet, which is called a rebate in Britain and Australia, serves as an element of joinery.

The front blade position on Stanley's No. 78 makes it a shoulder plane, but it is primarily used as a rabbeting fillister with the iron in the rear position. Easy to find used, the nicker or the fence are often missing.

Stanley Tools

As such, the edge of the board, in essence, becomes a tongue. A rabbet can also be used to reduce the thickness of an edge so that it will fit in a groove, as in the case of a trapped panel, or perhaps the back of a cabinet.

The No. 78, originally called a "duplex fillister and rabbet" plane—has been made by Stanley Tools for one hundred and thirty years. Today, the company calls it their 12-078 Duplex Rebate Plane. It has two cutter positions—one for making

A depth control adjustment with a thumbscrew is located on the right side of the plane between the two cutters, and this stop determines how deep the rabbet will be.

An adjustable fence controls the width of the cut. The fence can be attached to the right or left side of the body, which comes in handy when the grain is running the wrong way and the stroke needs to follow it.

rabbets and the other for bull-nose work (more on this in a minute). Between the two cutters is a depth control adjustment that determines the depth of the rabbet. An adjustable fence controls the width of the cut, and a cutting spur (called a nicker) scores cross grain ahead of the cutter to minimize tear-out. The fence can be switched from the right to the left of the plane, in case the grain is running the wrong way and the plane needs to change direction. The iron is 1½" wide, which allows you to cut just about any rabbet you might need.

The No. 78 is referred to as "duplex" because the iron can be used amidships for rabbeting, or it can be moved up front and used as a bull-nose plane to clean out the ends of cuts. It is referred to as a "fillister"

A three-headed cutting spur (called a nicker) scores cross grain ahead of the cutter to minimize tear-out. The fourth spur is missing, as no scoring cut is needed in long grain so the nicker can be rotated out of use.

because that is the traditional name for a plane that cuts rabbets and has both depth and width adjustment controls.

There is a lever cap but no cap iron on a No. 78. The lever cap is a cast iron plate that holds the iron in place, but it has no chipbreaker. A dome-head machine screw holds the lever cap to the plane body, and a small thumbscrew (or, on some models a round nickel-coated knob) provides tension. A long lever ends near the top of the tote and is used to adjust the height of the iron (and, of course, the thickness of the shaving). This lever, which was added to the design in the 1920s, locks into a series of shallow grooves in the bottom of the iron.

The depth of cut control (called a depth stop) on the right hand side of the plane is nothing more than a 2" long fence with a slot in it that allows it to slide up and down. There is no mechanical control for micro-adjustments. The depth stop is simply set by opening and closing a thumbscrew.

Behind the depth stop is a small wheel with a couple of spurs on it. The spurs can be sharpened and rotated into use, one at a time. The spur is set at the inside of the cut and slices through the face of stock cross-grain so that the iron's passage won't cause tear-out. The spur hits the wood half

A long lever on top of the plane locks into a series of shallow grooves in the bottom of the iron, thereby allowing the user to easily adjust the thickness of the shaving.

an inch ahead of the iron. There is a gap where one of the four spurs would be on the wheel, and this setting is used when working long grain and no nicker is necessary.

Using a No. 78

This plane is simple to set up and use. Once the iron has been properly sharpened to a standard 25° with a small secondary bevel, set it for a very thin cut. Lock the fence in position to cut the full width of the desired rabbet. If the rabbet will be milled across the grain, rotate a nicker to the down position. Set the depth stop for a shallow cut (about ⅛" deep), for now. If the cut is across grain, it's a good idea to clamp waste stock across the end of the cut to prevent tear-out.

Although it can be used left-handed, this is essentially a right-hand tool. So, the following instructions are for a right-handed user. Begin the cut by grasping the tote in the right hand. It feels comfortable to extend the index finger along the right side of the tool, resting it on the body close to the top of the iron. Slide the

An aggressive cut can be hard to control. Lock the fence for the full width of the desired rabbet, and adjust the depth stop to take thin shavings. Engage a nicker if the cut is across grain, such as when milling a tenon.

thumb of the left hand into the triangle formed by the front frog and the bull-nose at the front of the plane. Lay the index finger of the left hand along the bottom of the fence so that it rides against the wood being planed.

Begin cutting the rabbet with short, even, gentle strokes that establish the perimeters. The nicker will shear the grain and define the cut, and the iron will begin to shave the top of the rabbet. If the cut along the grain is too thick or too thin, change the depth of the iron by opening the thumbscrew on the lever cap slightly, and then pressing up or down on the lever. The cut is too thick if it chips rather than slices. On cross-grain cuts, it's a good idea to score the outline of the rabbet with a steel straightedge and a sharp utility knife. Surprisingly, you can usually take a deeper cut across the grain than with it. That's because the cross-grain shavings are very short, so tear-out isn't the problem that one might expect . . . in large part thanks to the nicker.

With the rabbet defined, the width can be checked. It's a good idea to do this after removing only a few thin shavings, rather than creating a full rabbet that is a little too narrow—when this happens, the No. 78 has a very difficult time removing a thin strip from the vertical wall of the rabbet (it tends to lean because of a lack of support). A shoulder plane with a clamped-on fence may be a better option. Lee Valley and others offer edge trimming planes for this task.

After confirming that the fence is set correctly, adjust the depth stop to allow the plane to cut the rabbet to its full depth. With the cut already defined and the iron set, make passes along the entire length of the rabbet using an even stroke throughout.

If the rabbet is to be stopped (that is, it meets a vertical wall before exiting at the other end of the board), stop the cut by clamping a small stop block of wood in place about 2½" past the planned end of the cut, and work right up to this stop on each pass. The extra couple of inches allows for the fact that the iron is about that far back from the front of the plane. In this case, the last shaving on each pass will need to be broken each time—using a sharp chisel helps. After the last pass is made, use the chisel to cut vertically down through the end of the rabbet. Then switch the iron on the No. 78 to its front (bull nose) position. Set it for a shallow cut and use the plane much like a chisel to clean out the corner. Very short strokes will do the job.

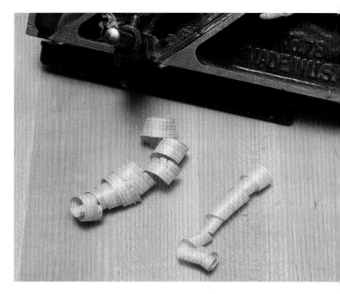

If the shavings are too thick (left), retard the iron by opening the thumbscrew on the lever cap slightly, pressing down on the lever, and then locking the iron in its new position.

When cutting rabbets across the grain, pre-cut the fibers near the surface to prevent tear-out. A sharp utility knife works well, allowing the plane to deliver short shavings instead of trying to follow the grain.

History of Hand Planes
Ohio Tool

This transitional company began in the heyday of wooden planes and made the switch to metal bodies rather successfully. It was incorporated in 1823 in Columbus, Ohio (about halfway between today's steel mills in Pittsburgh and Gary, Indiana), and merged with P. Hayden & Co. in 1851. In 1893, it was combined with Auburn Tool, and between those years Ohio Tool became a major manufacturer of hand planes and other tools. The steel planes were very similar to Stanley's, and the wooden lines included window, molding and plow planes. Much of the work was performed by prison labor under contract with the state's penal system.

Martin Donnelley / mjdtools.com

The Stanley No. 190

Often described as a less useful and less desirable version of the No. 78, the readily available No. 190 rabbet plane was made from the 1880s to the 1960s. It looks very much like its cousin except that it isn't a duplex plane. That is, there is only one place to bed the iron instead of two. It also lacks the No. 78's fence, but it does have the depth stop and nicker.

Stanley's No. 190 rabbet plane isn't a duplex (there's only one position for the iron), and it was designed to work with a clamped-on fence instead of a built-in fence.

Both planes use the same iron (1½" wide), and replacements are readily available. In fact, Lie-Nielsen sells a ⅛" thick replacement blade that fits either plane, and it's a significant upgrade. If more than one iron is on hand, the cutting edges can be ground to different widths (½", ¾" and 1", for example), and the plane can then be used with a clamped-on fence to cut or clean dadoes ¼" deep. Otherwise, it can be used to cut rabbets up to 1½" wide, using a fence clamped to the work.

The most critical part of a plane is the iron (blade). A good iron in a poor plane will perform a lot better than a poor iron in a good plane. Most inexpensive planes can be dramatically upgraded by replacing this one part of the tool with a superior version, such as the ones shown below from Lee Valley. Almost every good furniture builder will eventually switch the irons in his or her old planes to heavier, thicker ones, but size is by no means the only measure of a superior blade. Steel is deceptive. It all looks the same. So, some other facets to consider are the chemical composition of the steel, its manufacturing process, and its hardness.

Lee Valley Tools Ltd.

In addition to replacing the actual blade, you also have the option of replacing the cap iron and chipbreaker. (See Chapter 7 for information on the various parts of a plane). Many planes come with a two-part blade system, the actual iron and a second piece of steel called a cap iron that is attached to it with a threaded flat or dome-head machine screw. Usually, the last ½" or so of the leading edge of the cap iron (nearest the bevel) has a downward curl to it, a curve that goes away from the iron for a bit and then returns right at the edge. The end of this curl is bent so that the leading edge sits back a little from the iron's edge, putting the cap iron under pressure when it is screwed tightly to the iron. The back of this leading edge is under-beveled slightly, creating a tight seal against the non-beveled face of the iron. This sealed edge is called the chipbreaker, and its

The chipbreaker forms a curve that breaks shavings as they travel through the mouth. The chipbreaker also makes the shavings curl so that they don't start a split in the wood ahead of the cutting edge.

function is to curl shavings up so that they break constantly. Breaking the shavings partly prevents the cutting edge from starting a split that follows the grain. It also allows the shavings to curl out of the mouth rather than becoming jammed.

When upgrading an iron to a heavier one, many woodworkers also like to upgrade the cap iron/ chip breaker, too. Heavier irons have essentially no flex in them, so they don't behave like the original, thin blades. A new, thicker cap iron will usually create a tighter seal with the new, heavy iron. It will also dampen vibration. Lie-Nielsen's replacement chipbreakers are ⅛" thick with a .015" lip ground at a 1° angle to provide excellent contact between the leading edge of the chip breaker and the blade.

Unfortunately, they are designed specifically for the company's tools; while it is possible that they may fit some original Stanley or Record planes, check with them before ordering. Hock Tools' chipbreakers are 3mm thick (0.118"), and they come with a knurled cap screw in 1¾" width for No. 3 planes, 2" for No. 4 and No. 5, 2⅜" for No. 6 and No. 7, and 2⅝" for the No. 8.

Thickness

Lie-Nielsen Toolworks makes replacement blades for both their own planes and some other manufacturers'. According to the company, their replacement blades for bench planes are thinner so they will fit the original Stanley, Record or other makers' bench planes: "If the blade is too thick, the yoke on your plane will not properly engage the slot in the chipbreaker, the chipbreaker screw may not be long enough to install the chipbreaker at all, (or) most importantly, the mouth opening may not be large enough to allow the blade, or a shaving, to pass." In most cases, their bench plane replacement blades are .095" thick.

Hock Tools supplies thick, heavy, high quality, chatter resistant replacement irons for virtually any size or shape of hand plane. Custom sizes can be ordered as well.

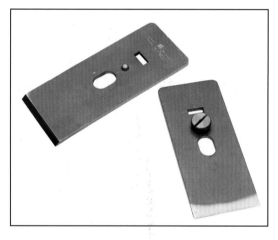

Immensely strong, Hock Tools' chipbreakers are just under ⅛" thick. Unlike traditional versions, they are not curled but milled perfectly flat so that they lock tightly to the iron without leaving any gaps.

Hock's replacement irons are 3/32" thick and "offer a substantial improvement over the inferior chrome-vanadium that comes with most new tools." They also claim that their high carbon steel blades can be honed "easier, and sharper."

Peck Tool Company offers a range of replacement irons and a few chipbreakers from Kunz, in Germany. Their orange colored irons are hardened to HR 65 and will fit Kunz, Stanley and similar planes. A company called Tools for Working Wood, which is located in New York, offers a line of replacement irons based on the work of noted infill plane builder and toolmaker Ray

Iles. Ray, a member of an old and respected Sheffield steel-working family, uses a D2 alloy in the cutters that he fabricates in Lincolnshire, England.

The venerable Lee Valley Toolworks offers high quality O1 and A2 alloy irons for Stanley and Record planes that are lapped on the back side to ²⁄₁₀₀₀". Their bench plane blades are 0.094" (³⁄₃₂") thick, which is 17% thicker than the industry standard of 0.080". All are 7" long, have a 30° bevel, and are compatible with a wide range of planes. Check with the company for specific sizing. Lee Valley blades for block planes are 0.125" (⅛") thick. Worth noting is that Lee Valley offers extra irons for several of the Veritas line of planes, including the low angle smoother and bevel up smoother, and these optional irons actually increase the angle of these planes. For working difficult grain, additional blades are available at 38° and 50° bevel, and when combined with the 12° bedding these raise the cut to 50° (York pitch) and 62° respectively.

Stanley Tools offers a full line of replacement irons for the planes they still make and market. Other manufacturers such as Primus, Bridge City, Ron Brese and others offer replacement irons specific to their planes. And Paul Williams of Academy Saws in Australia adds another twist: his replacement irons are slightly bent, to add tension and reduce chatter when attached to the cap iron. They are also a little harder than most U.S. blades. Paul specializes in Bailey-style plane irons.

Hardness

Lie-Nielsen's irons are relatively hard, scoring between 60 and 62 on the Rockwell scale. Tool steel's hardness is measured on a benchtop machine that drops a very hard steel ball or a pointed diamond onto it, and then measures the depth of the depression left behind. The gradations are known as the Rockwell scale,

Installing Hock's high carbon replacement irons in standard bench planes offers substantial improvement over the chrome-vanadium cutter that comes with most new tools. The heavy irons virtually eliminate chatter.

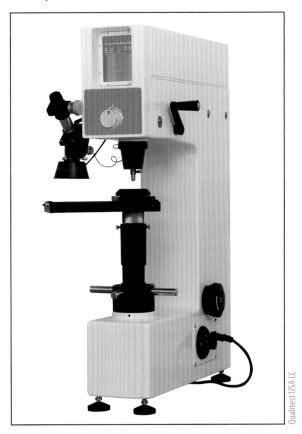

Qualitest USA LC

A machine is used to determine the hardness of tool steel by hitting it with a steel ball or a pointed diamond, measuring the depth of the depression, and then expressing this in terms of the Rockwell scale of hardness.

so named because the machine was invented in 1914 by Connecticut engineers Hugh and Stanley Rockwell. There is a delicate balance between hard and brittle. If steel is too hard, the leading edge of a blade will chip and fragment under impact. Think of the way a carbide saw tip shatters when it meets an old nail during a cut. On the other hand, if an iron is too soft, it won't hold an edge. Good kitchen cutlery will range from about HRC 56 to HRC 62. A typical wood axe will be rated about HRC 43, and a bench chisel will generally be in the low 50s. There are various Rockwell scales for different metals and other materials, but tool steel is generally measured on the C scale, where a 120° diamond cone is used to indent the metal at a pressure of 150 kgf. The acronym "kgf" means kilogram-force, and in layman's terms that is the amount of force exerted on one kilogram of mass by Earth's gravity.

The balance between malleable and brittle has another angle to it. Ron Hock (metalworker and owner of Hock Tools in Fort Bragg, California) points out that the trade-off can be expressed in terms of three properties: the ability to hold an edge, the ease of sharpening that edge, or its resistance to corrosion. A toolmaker can only deliver two of those three, and Ron feels that, in woodworking, corrosion resistance is the least important. He prefers an edge that is easily sharpened

History of Hand Planes
Edward Preston and Sons Ltd.

Founded in Birmingham, England in 1825, Preston made planes, rules and other wood-working tools until the company became part of Record Tools in 1932. Known for innovative and high quality products such as the No. 1369 Adjustable Side Rabbet Plane, Preston eventually became one of Britain's leading tool manufacturers. Their catalogue ran to more than two hundred pages, listing over 1,000 products. Preston's famous logo, the Birds Eye, was registered as a trademark in 1876.

From a craftsman's point of view, Preston's major contributions to woodworking history were their cast iron shoulder, rabbet, and side-rabbet planes, all of which continued (in simpler forms) to be manufactured by Record Tools after the takeover.

George Radion / htpaa.org.au

and long lasting, and most woodworkers would agree. Hock's blades, like those of Lie-Nielsen, run a bit harder than most (HRC 62), which means they will last a long time. He also points out that they are not as hard or brittle as most Japanese blades, which means that sharpening isn't difficult.

In cryogenics, tools such as plane irons and chisels are frozen to extreme temperatures in a vat-like refrigerator. Proponents believe that tools treated this way will keep an edge for twice as long as normal.

Japanese blades are laminated. A thin layer of very hard steel is bonded to a thick layer of soft steel or even iron, and the back of the blade (the hard side) is then hollowed. That leaves less of the high-grade steel to sharpen. If the blades weren't hollow, woodworkers would have to grind away a great deal of very hard metal to flatten the back of the blade. Instead, they only have to touch up a thin band of hard steel on the bevel.

Cryogenics

Cryogenics has been around for quite some time, and the word evokes a sense of science fiction. It has been used in connection with the theory that a diseased human could be instantly frozen while still alive, and woken up some centuries later when humanity has discovered a cure for the affliction. In more practical terms, it's a branch of physics that studies how to produce and maintain extremely low temperatures, and how various elements and compounds behave at those extremes. It uses the Kelvin scale, which is the same scale used to measure the color of light (or more specifically, the temperature of light, which can be discovered by examining its color). Photographers have long known that daylight is in the vicinity of 5500K, and from there warm light is red while cold light is blue.

Proponents of cryogenics believe that cooling some metals to incredible temperatures lower than -300°F can help them keep an edge for twice as long as similar tools that haven't been subjected to the process.

As a commercially available service, cryogenically freezing tools first became popular in the 1970s. At the time, most major tool manufacturers frankly thought it was a crackpot idea, and the rough and ready manner in which it was practiced bolstered their arguments by destroying a lot of good tools. There has been a learning curve, and the ensuing decades have produced a lot of evidence that the process, properly controlled, can produce some very encouraging results.

One believer in the new generation of cryogenics is Ron Hock. "After considerable research and evaluation," he says, "I decided to add A2 replacement blades to our catalog. We're offering the nine most popular replacement sizes in AISI A2 that has been cryogenically treated for maximum edge retention. A2 differs from our usual High Carbon Steel with the addition of significant amounts of chromium and molybdenum. While 'stainless' amounts of chromium (12% or more) make tool steel 'gummy' and hard to sharpen, the modest amount of chromium in A2 (5%) improves its toughness and abrasion resistance, but imparts only a slight measure of corrosion resistance (like high carbon steel, it will rust, and appropriate preventative care must be taken). A2 is one of the steels that respond well to cryogenic treatment. This extreme cold treatment (-320°F) increases the steel's toughness without any decrease in hardness. You get increased wear resistance without any increase in brittleness so a cryogenically treated blade will hold its edge longer. You can keep working, instead of sharpening."

Lie-Nielsen Toolworks have traditionally used water-quenched steel (W-1 grade, the "W" signifying water). However, they have now changed to A-2 steel, "because our research convinces us that cryogenically treated A-2 will hold an edge significantly longer if properly done. It can still be sharpened with conventional abrasives, while some other special alloys can't." A-2 steel is a cold-worked, air-hardened medium alloy that delivers a superior cutting edge akin to the quality of a Hock blade. Lie-Nielsen freezes this alloy cryogenically to -320°F for twenty hours, and then tempers it twice to achieve the ideal hardness.

Other high quality iron suppliers including Bridge City and Knight Toolworks also now offer cryogenically treated blades. The consensus among the best toolmakers seems to be that this technology has finally come of age and is a valuable and trustworthy process.

History of Hand Planes
Record Tools

Yet one more British key to the history of planes, Record is similar in many ways to the American company Stanley. It was founded in 1898 by two brothers, and was originally called C & J Hampton Limited. The product line included roofing tools, vises, clamps and other hand tools. Within a decade the factory had moved to Sheffield's steel mills, and registered Record as a trademark.

In 1931, the company introduced eleven hand planes including block, smoothing, jack, fore and jointer models. They were very close copies of Stanley's Bailey line, and this was possible because Stanley's original patent had by now expired.

In 1934, the Record parent company (C & J Hampton Limited) purchased the rights to the hand plane designs of Edward Preston & Sons, Ltd. These includes rabbet, bull-nose and shoulder planes, which expanded the Record line and gave the firm a comprehensive catalog.

In 1964, Record bought half of William Marples & Sons, Ltd., and nine years later it merged with Ridgeway to become Record Ridgeway Tools Ltd. Today, it is part of the Irwin group of companies.

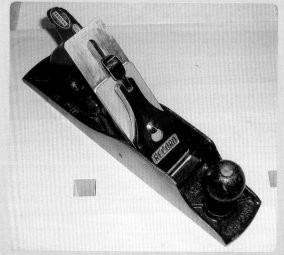

Wayne Cox

History of Hand Planes
Sargent Manufacturing Co.

In 1857, three brothers named Sargent purchased Peck & Walter Manufacturing in New Britain, Connecticut and shortly thereafter moved the plant to New Haven. By the outbreak of war in Europe in 1914, Sargent Mfg. was one of the largest hardware factories in America. After the Second World War, the company began to specialize in door and window hardware. They also began to copy many of the Stanley plane models as soon as the original patents ran out during the 1930s, and eventually became the second largest maker of hand planes in the U.S.

In the 1960s, Sargent began a merger and ownership cycle that ended up in 1996 with their acquisition by ASSA ABLOY of Sweden.

Scott Dobek / dustynewt.com

Chemical Composition of Steel

Iron used to be turned into tool steel by rolling it and breaking and re-making the chemical bonds within the compound so that a relatively soft material eventually became hard. That cold rolling process is still used in some industries, but toolmakers generally work steel with heat in extremely hot furnaces.

When iron is being turned into steel, the mill can change the nature of the finished product by adding various other metals to control certain properties. When a secondary element is added, the steel becomes an alloy. Common hardeners such as vanadium and tungsten are familiar terms because toolmakers mention them often in their marketing. Another element, molybdenum, has an extremely high melting point and

Mechanics are accustomed to seeing marketing claims that list common steel hardeners such as chrome, vanadium and tungsten in their tools. Woodworkers can benefit from them, as well, when buying plane irons.

it is used to form carbides, which in turn lend a lot of strength to steel. A carbide is a compound that contains carbon along with one or more elements that have a lesser electro-negative ability (that is, an atom's ability to attract electrons in a covalent bond). Niobium is another element used in tool steel alloys, but it is more commonly found in high-pressure pipelines and similar applications. As a strengthening agent in an alloy, it is usually a very small part of the mix (less than one-tenth of one per cent).

One of the most important corrosion fighting elements added to steel is chrome. At higher concentrations (above 11.5% by weight), it creates stainless steel. When combined with vanadium, it becomes chrome-vanadium high-speed tool steel. Unfortunately, this hard compound is difficult to sharpen using conventional woodshop methods, so a better choice is a high carbon steel with lower levels of hardeners. Hock Tools use a high carbon tool steel that is 0.95% carbon, and the company believes that this "delivers the finest, sharpest edge possible. Its chromium and vanadium additions amount to only 0.5% each, allowing quick, clean honing with traditional techniques. High-carbon steel holds and takes an edge better than anything else."

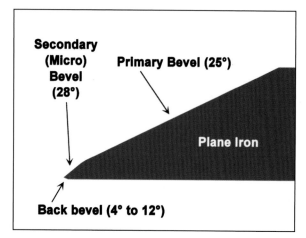

A small secondary (micro) bevel can be touched up on a fine-grit honing stone in only a few seconds. It's much faster than having to regrind the entire bevel each time it dulls.

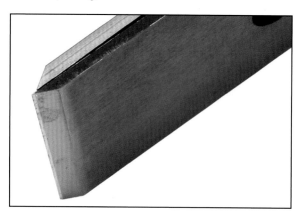

For difficult grain, some experienced woodworkers grind a primary bevel, add a micro bevel, and then hone a small bevel on the back (flat) side of the iron, to increase shear.

Physical Properties

The shape of a cutting edge is important, too. The vast majority of plane irons are sold as squared-off steel rectangles with a single beveled edge. Sometimes a secondary bevel is added at the factory, but almost always this is done in the woodshop after the plane reaches its new home. Either the tool works or the new owner can customize irons with a crowned edge or even a back bevel. And for rough work, there are serrated or "toothed" irons.

A primary bevel on most planes is ground at 25°, and it's generally a good idea to add a small secondary bevel at 27° or 28°. Then, as the edge wears, it can be touched up on a fine-grit honing stone in a few seconds, rather than having to regrind the entire bevel each time.

A back bevel is a small bevel ground on the trailing face of the iron (what is usually the flat back), and it can be up to 12° in severity, but is usually less. A back bevel can help control tear-out in highly figured wood. It is a technique borrowed from power planers (or perhaps the borrowing was the other way around).

A crown is a slow gentle curve across the entire width of the cutting edge, designed to

Lee Valley Tools Ltd.

Toothed irons (blades with a geometric serration along the cutting edge) are far more aggressive than standard irons. They are designed to flatten high spots and remove lots of waste quickly.

stop the corners of an iron from leaving trails in the wood. Sometimes only the last small segment at each side of the edge is rounded, and most of the iron is still straight across. Severe crowning is usually reserved for scrub planes.

Serrated (toothed) irons are designed to remove a lot of material quickly. Lie-Nielsen offers two varieties. Their scrapers have a V-shaped tooth, and their bench planes have a series of small, square teeth. "In the scraper, they are used to rough up a surface, either as a prep for veneering, and left as is; or to work down an area of difficult grain, after which the regular scraper blade is used. In bench and block planes, they are used to work areas of difficult grain by planing diagonally across from one direction, and then diagonally from the other direction. After that, the regular smoothing blade is used. The toothed blades reduce tear-out, and the regular blade can usually finish the job (or you would switch to the scraper). Both types leave a rough surface." The company has noted that luthiers find these irons especially useful in the bench and block planes.

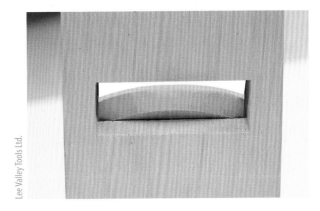

Lee Valley Tools Ltd.

The idea behind crowning irons (creating a gentle arc along the cutting edge) is that overlapping strokes won't leave grooves. Scrub planes take this concept to an extreme, using a deep crown to remove lots of wood.

Among the toothed (serrated) irons offered by Lee Valley are lapped blades for their bevel up planes. These are ³⁄₁₆" (0.187") thick, in either A2 or O1 tool steel. The standard 38° blade is 2¼" wide tool steel hardened to Rc60-62, and this is the same size as their other bevel-up planes, allowing blades of various bevel angles to be interchanged between planes.

The Blum Blade System

Gary Blum is a toolmaker located in Walnut, Iowa, which is about 45 miles east of Omaha. His company, which can be found online at **BlumToolCo. com**, has done something quite dramatic in hand plane design. A custom furniture builder with decades of experience in joinery and cabinetmaking, Gary decided that standard wooden plane irons were too light, and too hard to sharpen. His revolutionary system overcomes most of the objections commonly made against wooden planes, and also displays many advantages when

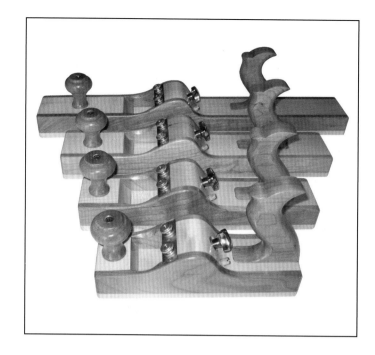

compared to metal planes. Instead of a large iron with a chipbreaker (cap iron), he uses a small, thin blade attached to a massive support block. Gary's passion has always been tools, especially antique planes. He has been a member of Mid-West Tool Collectors for more than thirty years, and his newest passion was especially influenced by working on job sites with tradesmen who were using tools (especially block planes) that were extremely dull. Once they saw him work, they would ask him to sharpen their plane irons.

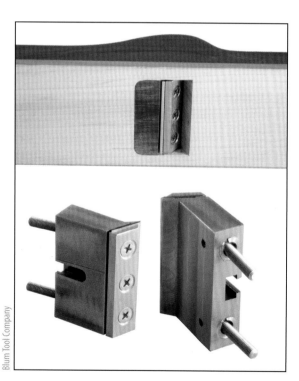

Blum Tool Company uses a massive blade holder and a small, disposable blade in their wooden bench planes. The system eliminates sharpening.

The Blum Tool Company system has a number of special features. Their planes are fully adjustable without tools, and there is no separate chipbreaker. The A-2 steel blades are small enough and inexpensive enough to be disposable, or they can be sharpened. Once installed, there is no separate lateral adjustment necessary. That is, the cutting edge is always parallel to the mouth opening.

Because of the way it's engineered, a Blum Tool Co. wooden plane doesn't suffer one of the oldest problems with bench planes. The mouth doesn't widen as the sole is worn down or trued up on a jointer. That's because the opening doesn't need to be wedge-shaped. Gary's planes glide across the work as only wood on wood can, and being made of wood, they don't rust. In addition to standard set-ups, he also offers a scraper frog, a cambered (slightly crowned) frog, and carbide blades.

History of Hand Planes

Stewart Spiers

Scotland has produced many superior plane makers and the town of Ayr, on the Firth of Clyde in the southwest corner, has had more than its fair share. Perhaps the most renowned of these, Spiers began his working life as a cabinetmaker and, given his inventive nature, soon began building his own hand planes. The first one he built was a rough casting that he purchased and re-worked, and then sold for an impressive fee to another cabinetmaker. By the mid 1860s, he was making nothing but planes, and concentrating on dovetailed infill versions. He had an eye for grace and proportion, and a sound knowledge of locally available metals, primarily steel and brass. His inquisitive mind led to many small improvements in the manufacturing process.

After his death, Spiers' three daughters took over the business and continued running it until the company was purchased in 1923 by John McFadyen, an engineer and hotelier.

Martin Donnelley / mjdtools.com

How It Works

The thin blade in a Blum plane is sandwiched between a massive frog which is ¾" thick at the bottom, and a back-up iron which is 5/32" thick. The leading edge of the frog thus becomes the chipbreaker and guides the shavings up and into the throat. The reverse angle of the frog matches the angle at the front of the throat, so the old problem of throat widening as the sole is trued or worn down is no longer an issue. In fact, a woodworker can take more than ⅜" off of the sole during the life of

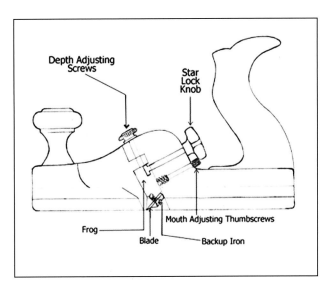

the plane, and the opening will still be the same.

The frog is adjusted for blade depth and lateral projection with two adjusting nuts at the top of the plane. By being situated at the outer sides of the frog, adjusting depth also controls lateral adjustment, so no separate lateral adjuster is required. This is a very fast and precise process.

There is one surprising side effect of angling the frog forward. On traditional planes, to take up backlash the blade is advanced downward before cutting, so one must guess how far the iron should protrude, then test it and make adjustments. On these planes, the opposite happens. The cutter is advanced and then pulled up to just the right setting. No guess work. Backlash is so minimal that adjustments can be made in either direction most of the time. The large star knob tightens the frog lock bolt, and this bolt is captured in a T-slot on the back of the frog. For normal planing, the knob just needs to be snug and doesn't need to be loosened to make depth adjustments. For very hard woods, it should be tightened more and loosened slightly before adjusting.

Small manufacturers such as Blum Tool Co. use great attention to detail to counteract their limited production ability. For example, the company offers several species options, such as the mesquite model shown here.

The mouth opening is adjustable without tools by turning two knurled thumbscrews that bear against the back of the frog. The blade is removed for sharpening by lowering the frog slightly below the sole and loosening the three screws in the back-up iron. The blade can then be slipped out, because it is slotted for the screws. Because of the thinness of the blade, honing (no grinding) will quickly restore a flat bevel. A normal honing guide will not work for so small a blade, so the company sells simple jigs for this, or one may also make a wooden jig patterned after theirs.

Blum Tool Co. offers a full line of smooth, jack, fore and jointer planes along with a wide variety of block planes and specialty planes.

A shooting board is a device that allows the woodworker to use a bench plane to make perfectly square cuts on the ends of boards; perfect jointing cuts along the edges of small boards; and perfect miters. They have been around a long time, so there is plenty of theory and argument about them. But everyone agrees that, when built properly and used well, they deliver better results than a power miter box or a miter gauge on the table saw. They are also a heck of a lot of fun to use.

What makes a shooting board work is that the cutting edge of a bench plane iron is not as wide as the sole of the plane. The small part of the sole outside the cutter runs against the side of a ramp and this thin strip of steel works like a stop. When the plane moves, it creates a small, thin rabbet along the side of the ramp. The depth of this rabbet is equal to the amount of the iron protruding through the sole.

The iron of a plane isn't as wide as the sole. The small amount of steel on either side of the mouth allows it to ride against a fence without digging in further than the depth of cut. This is the secret of shooting boards.

A cleat attached to the underside of the shooting board is trapped in a vise during use. This prevents the board from moving about when parts are being worked.

Building a Ramped Shooting Board

The following jig is built for right-handed woodworkers, and left-handed folks will be more comfortable if they build a mirror image of it. The first element of a shooting board is a base (A) that has a cleat (B) on the bottom that works like a bench hook and can be locked into a vise to secure the jig. Some woodworkers prefer to just rest the cleat against the side of the bench, but having it secured by a vise makes the operation more secure. Cut the base to size from ¾" thick hardwood or plywood (see the Parts List on page 102 for dimensions), and

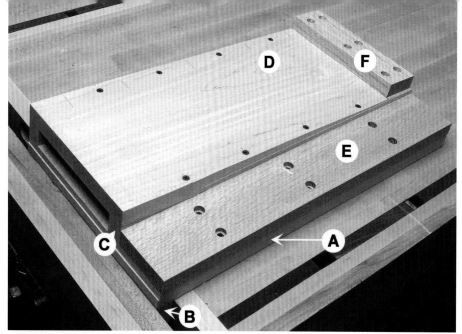

Parts List
A. Base: ¾" x 10¾" x 20"
B. Cleat: ¾" x 1½" x 10¾"
C. Wedge: ¾" x 1" x 20"
D. Ramp: ¾" x 7¾" x 20"
E. Runway: ¾" x 3" x 20"
F. Fence: ¾" x 2⅛" x 7½"

The main surface of the shooting board is a ramp sloping toward the fence. This is attached to the base by a pair of wedges. The slope allows the plane iron's cutting edge to wear evenly and cut at a mild skew.

Two tapered wedges are attached to the base with screws and glue, and the ramp lies upon these. The idea here is that the ramp holds the wood at a slight angle, allowing the plane iron to wear more evenly.

A hardwood runway is attached to the jig to one side of the ramp (on the right side for right-handed woodworkers), and the plane rests upon this runway as it slides back and forth.

screw the cleat to it using pre-drilled, counter-bored pilot holes to avoid splitting the wood. It's a good idea to clamp parts together when drilling pilot holes and driving screws.

Next, two wedges (C) are attached to the top of the base. These are cut on the band saw and then the rough edges are planed smooth. Clamp both wedges to the bench while planing, and they'll be the same thickness when you're done. Secure them to the base with glue and five screws each, driven into countersunk, pre-drilled pilot holes. Note that the screws at the lower end are shorter than those at the higher end, and one of the cleats is set in three inches from the edge.

Cut the ramp (D) to size next, and secure it to the tops of the cleats using glue and four screws in each, again driving them into countersunk and pre-drilled pilot holes. Make sure the heads are slightly below the surface of the ramp. The idea behind the ramp is that, in use, the plane iron will wear more evenly, and it will also address the work at a slightly skewed angle, which helps it to slice through end grain.

With the ramp in place, measure and then cut a board for the runway (E). This should be a hard-wearing species such as hard maple or oak, as the plane will travel along it. Secure the runway with six screws driven into counter-bored, pre-drilled pilot holes. Don't glue it in place as it may need to be replaced sometime.

The last element in the shooting board is the fence (F). Mark its location on the ramp by using a square to draw a line at exactly 90° to the edge of the ramp that lies next to the runway. This is critical. Cut the fence to size, and then clamp it to the ramp before drilling counter-bored pilot holes for six screws. Check again with the square before screwing the fence in place with just two of the screws. The fence shouldn't be glued in place, as it will need to be adjusted in a minute.

It's crucial that the fence lies at exactly 90° to the plane's sole when placed against the edge of the ramp (or at 45° on a board made for shooting miters). The fence is screwed but not glued in place.

Using the Shooting Board

The first step here is to check that the fence is square. Place the plane (with the iron retarded) on the runway, so that it is tight against the ramp. Use a try square, machinist's square or metal triangle to check that the fence lies at exactly 90° to the bottom (sole) of the plane. Note that we're not relying on the runway edge here. The reading from the sole of the plane will be more accurate than one taken from the edge of the ramp. If any adjustment is needed, clamp the fence to the ramp, loosen one of the two screws, and gently tap the fence into position with a small hammer. Install the other four screws before re-installing the one you removed.

There will be some slight tear-out at the end of each cut. There are two ways to deal with this. A scrap piece that is absolutely

Don't clamp the work to the shooting board. Just hold it tightly against the fence, and slide it forward after each pass. Taking a light cut and placing a scrap behind the workpiece helps control tear-out.

parallel can be placed against the fence as shown, or one can back-chamfer the end of the cut. This simply means taking a couple of partial passes to create a short chamfer, and then flipping the board so that the chamfer is now at the end of the cut.

Set the plane for a minimum cut. Any sharp, tuned plane with high sides that are at true right angles to the sole will work, but heavier planes work better. Some woodworkers prefer a long plane, many like a jack, and my personal favorite is my Lie-Nielsen low angle smoother.

Hold-downs are not a great idea with shooting boards. The idea is that a pass is made, the work is moved forward, another pass is made, and so on. Having to lock down the work between passes would interfere with the rhythmic flow of the sequence.

The cut on a shooting board is very minimal, so there is little force required to move the plane. If there is resistance, reduce the depth of cut. Using too much force tends to let the outer

History of Hand Planes
Stanley Rule and Level Company

A giant in the industry, Henry Stanley founded the company in 1857 from an amalgam of earlier Stanley family enterprises and some unrelated businesses. In 1920, The Rule and Level Company merged with The Stanley Works and would go on to become its famous Hand Tools Division. Between 1857 and 1920, the Stanley Works made hardware and the Rule and Level company made tools, and they were separate entities although they shared some Directors and an amiable relationship.

Throughout those 63 years, the Rule and Level firm acquired most of its competitors to create the country's largest and most diversified manufacturer of hand tools. Among the acquisitions were three entities that had been owned by Leonard Bailey, and consequently many of the forty or so patents awarded to this genius became the property of Stanley. Their in-house engineer, Justus Traut, also earned numerous patents that related to planes and their construction, but the heart and soul of the planes business was the work of Bailey.

For more than one hundred and fifty years, Stanley has led the mass market portion of the hand planes industry, producing a complete and comprehensive line of tools that addressed the changing needs of a growing America and a large European market, too. They set the standard for working bench planes and it has been followed by countless other manufacturers. Today, Stanley is a worldwide supplier of hand tools and hardware, along with doors and other home construction products.

edge of the plane ride up off the runway, and the cut is then no longer at 90°. For this reason, planes with higher sides work better. Wooden planes require more pressure than those with cast iron bodies, simply because of the difference in their weights.

The first time a plane is used on a shooting board, it takes small shavings from the ramp until the edge of the sole bottoms out. This is also true when the depth of cut is changed, or when a different plane is used that has less metal between the edge of the iron and the edge of the sole.

Occasional waxing of the sole of the plane and the top of the runway will reduce friction and allow the plane to glide more easily. I like to use clear neutral show polish, which I wipe on, allow to dry, and then polish with a soft, clean rag. It is a hard coating that won't transfer to the work and interfere with glue or finish.

Index